HIMMLISCH
SONNE, MOND UND STERNE
IM SCHMUCK

HEAVENLY
THE SUN, MOON AND STARS
IN JEWELLERY

Jewellery

Order
Universe
Cosmos
Κόσμος
Kosmos
Universum
Ordnung
Schmuck

FRITZ FALK

HIMMLISCH
SONNE, MOND UND STERNE
IM SCHMUCK

HEAVENLY
THE SUN, MOON AND STARS
IN JEWELLERY

SCHMUCKMUSEUM PFORZHEIM

arnoldsche

INHALT / CONTENTS

6 VORWORT
Cornelie Holzach
7 FOREWORD
Cornelie Holzach

8 SONNE, MOND UND STERNE – EINE EINFÜHRUNG
9 THE SUN, MOON AND STARS – AN INTRODUCTION
8 Alte Mythologien
11 Ancient mythologies
16 Judentum, Christentum und Islam
19 Judaism, Christianity and Islam
18 Heraldik und politische Symbole
19 Heraldry and political symbols
22 Auszeichnung
21 Distinction
24 Bildende Kunst
25 Fine art
26 Bühnenbild
29 Stage design
28 Musik
29 Music
30 Literatur
31 Literature
36 Kunsthandwerk
39 Artefacts and applied arts

46 ÄGPYTEN
47 EGYPT

50 ALTER ORIENT
53 THE ANCIENT NEAR EAST

58 KRETA, GRIECHENLAND UND ROM
61 CRETE, GREECE AND ROME

68 ETRURIEN
69 ETRURIA

72 VÖLKERWANDERUNGSZEIT, MITTELALTER UND RENAISSANCE
73 THE MIGRATION PERIOD, THE MIDDLE AGES, AND THE RENAISSANCE

78 BAROCKZEIT
79 THE BAROQUE ERA

86 19. JAHRHUNDERT
87 THE NINETEENTH CENTURY
86 Sonne, Mond und Sterne werden gesellschaftsfähig
89 The sun, moon and stars in high society
102 Rückbezug auf historische Vorbilder
105 The return to historical models
110 Fabergé und die Gestirne
109 Fabergé and the heavenly bodies
114 Sonne und Mond im volkstümlichen Schmuck
115 Sun and moon in folkloric jewellery

116	ART NOUVEAU	170	Amerika
119	ART NOUVEAU	171	The Americas
120	Das Sonnenmotiv		
119	The sun motif	172	UHREN
126	Sterne und Mondsicheln	175	WATCHES
129	Stars and crescent moon	172	Sonnenuhren
		175	Sundials
132	20. UND 21. JAHRHUNDERT	176	Astronomische Uhren
135	TWENTIETH AND TWENTY-FIRST CENTURIES	175	Astronomical clocks
		176	Anhänger-, Taschen- und Armbanduhren
138	Schmuck von bildenden Künstlern	177	Pocket-, pendant- and wristwatches
137	Jewellery by famous painters		
138	Schmuckkunst seit den 1950er-Jahren		
137	Art jewellery since the 1950s	186	Dank
154	Die Schmuckindustrie	186	Acknowledgements
155	The jewellery industry	187	Literatur in Auswahl
156	Berühmte Edelsteine	187	Selected bibliography
157	Famous precious stones		
		190	Bildnachweis
158	AUSSEREUROPÄISCHE KULTUREN	190	Photo credits
161	NON-EUROPEAN CULTURES		
162	Arabische Welt		
161	The Arab world		
162	Türkei, Kaukasus und Zentralasien		
167	Turkey, the Caucasus and central Asia		
164	Südostasien und Indonesien		
167	South East Asia and Indonesia		
168	Westafrika		
171	West Africa		

VORWORT

Vom unermesslich Großen zum überschaubar Kleinen – so wandern Sonnen, Monde und Sterne aus dem Universum in die delikaten und zierlichen Schmuckstücke, ob sie nun am Körper getragen werden, als hochfeine Objekte der Goldschmiedekunst oder als Werke der Kunst aus allen Epochen in diesem Buch versammelt sind. Viele davon sind auch in der Ausstellung zu sehen, die dieses kenntnisreiche und das Thema von den frühesten Anfängen bis in unsere Zeit geradezu enzyklopädisch behandelnde Buch begleitet. Ausstellung und Buch sind das Ergebnis einer lang gehegten Idee Fritz Falks, der sich mit Beharrlichkeit, umfangreicher Recherchearbeit und nicht zuletzt großer Freude an die vielschichtige Thematik der „Gestirne auf Erden" gemacht hat. Es scheint, als seien sie allgegenwärtig, denn in fast allen polytheistischen Religionen sind Gottheiten, die mit Sonne oder Mond in Verbindung stehen oder sie symbolisieren, vertreten. Selbst das Christentum hat seinen Stern: Mit dem Leitstern von Bethlehem werden die Heiligen Drei Könige auf den richtigen Weg geschickt. Allumfassend in ihrer Bedeutung oder unscheinbar in ihrer Gestalt wurden Sonne, Mond und Sterne Begleiter der Menschen in allen Epochen unserer Geschichte. Sie werden gefürchtet, geschätzt, geliebt – die Spannbreite ist groß, und die Vielfältigkeit kaum zu überschauen. Umso hilfreicher ist ein Buch wie dieses, es sortiert und belegt, lässt den Leser stöbern und macht ihn neugierig auf die unzähligen Darstellungen in Schmuck und Kunst. Oft sind sie nur zu erahnen, manchmal beherrschen sie den Gegenstand, und so ist dieses Buch auch ein Leitfaden durch die Ausstellung. Was in der Vergrößerung sichtbar wird, ist mitunter im Schmuckstück nur sehr klein zu sehen. Spektakuläre Schmuckstücke wiederum entfalten ihre wahre Pracht erst in der Ausstellung und erwecken dort größtmögliche Bewunderung und vielleicht auch Begehrlichkeiten. Buch und Ausstellung – beides konnte ermöglicht werden in nicht gerade einfachen Zeiten für die Stadt Pforzheim. Wir alle sind dankbar, dass es gelungen ist. Von Herzen gedankt sei Fritz Falk, der uns mitnimmt auf eine erkenntnisreiche und kurzweilige Reise durch das Universum – im Kleinen wie im Großen.

Cornelie Holzach
Leiterin des Schmuckmuseums Pforzheim

FOREWORD

From immeasurably large to manageably small – suns, moons and stars migrate from the universe into exquisitely delicate pieces of jewellery, which, whether worn on the body, as superlative objects bearing witness to the goldsmith's craft or as artworks from all eras, are collected in this book. Many of these pieces are also to be seen in the exhibition that this knowledgeably written book accompanies. Covering the subject from the earliest beginnings on down to the present in a truly encyclopaedic survey, the exhibition and the book are the result of an idea long cherished by Fritz Falk, who has approached the multifaceted subject of 'heavenly bodies on earth' with persistence, extensive research and, not least, irresistible enthusiasm. They seem to be everywhere because almost all polytheistic religions have deities associated with the sun or moon or symbolising them. Even Christianity has its star: guided by the Star of Bethlehem, the Three Kings were set on the right path. All-encompassing in significance or inconspicuous in appearance, the sun, moon and stars have accompanied us in all periods of our history. They are feared, appreciated, loved – the range is vast and the diversity staggering. Hence a book like this one is a great help because it sorts out and verifies, leaving readers free to browse and to whet their curiosity about the countless representations in jewellery and art. Often the heavenly bodies are only suggested, but at times they dominate the object, and so this book is also a guide through the exhibition. What becomes visible in magnification is sometimes so small in a piece of jewellery that it is very difficult to see in actual size. Spectacular pieces of jewellery, on the other hand, display their true magnificence once they are in the exhibition, where they arouse the greatest admiration and perhaps also secret feelings of covetousness. The book and the exhibition – both have been made possible at a time when things are not all that easy for the city of Pforzheim. We are thankful that this undertaking has been a success. To Fritz Falk we express our heartfelt thanks for taking us on such an insightful and entertaining journey through the universe – on a microcosmic and on a macrocosmic scale.

Cornelie Holzach
Director,
Pforzheim Jewellery Museum

SONNE, MOND UND STERNE – EINE EINFÜHRUNG

Ob im Alten Orient oder bei den Ägyptern, ob im antiken und christlichen Europa oder in den Kulturen des präkolumbischen Amerika, ob in Afrika, in Asien oder in Australien: Überall verband man Gottheiten mit der Sonne, dem Mond und den Sternen – oder sah in ihnen göttliche Zeichen am Himmel. Überall wurden sie verehrt, aber auch gefürchtet. Denn in den magischen, mythologischen und religiösen Vorstellungen der Menschen galten die Gestirne einerseits als Bewahrer des Glücks und des Wohlstands, andererseits als Boten und Träger böser Mächte.

Von der Antike bis zur Gegenwart huldigten Dichter, Komponisten und Maler den Himmelskörpern. Und Kunsthandwerker erfanden Preziosen aus Gold, Silber, Elfenbein und vielen anderen kostbaren Werkstoffen, mit denen sie die Kräfte und Mächte der Gestirne darstellten und beschworen.

Alte Mythologien
Die Menschen gaben den Gestirnen Namen. Im alten Ägypten kannte man den Sonnengott Re beziehungsweise Ra, der in zahlreichen Darstellungsformen überliefert ist. Als Mondgott wurden Iah und vor allem der Ibis-köpfige Thot verehrt, der auch als Pavian mit der Mondsichel auf dem Kopf dargestellt wurde (Abb. 5). Im 14. vorchristlichen Jahrhundert schuf der Pharao Echnaton mit der Verehrung des Sonnengotts Aton die wohl erste monotheistische Religion (Abb. 1).

Schamasch nannte man den Sonnengott bei den Assyrern und Babyloniern, wo die Hauptgottheit Marduk auch als „untergehende Sonne" bezeichnet wurde. Als Mondgott wurde Sin verehrt. Darüber hinaus gab es in der babylonischen Mythologie eine Mondgöttin namens Annit. In Sumer wurde Utu – der Sohn des Mondgottes Nanna – als Sonnengott verehrt, die Hethiter kannten die Sonnengöttin von Arinna. In den zoroastrischen Mythen erscheint Mah beziehungsweise Mãonghah

1 Hausaltar mit Echnaton, Nofretete und drei ihrer Töchter unter dem Strahlenaton, Amarna, Ägypten, 18. Dynastie, 14. Jh. v. Chr., Kalkstein, 33,5 × 39,5 × 3,5 cm. Family altar with Akhenaten, Nefertiti and three of their daughters under a radiant sun disc, Amarna, Egypt, 18th dynasty, 14th century BC, limestone, 33.5 × 39.5 × 3.5 cm. Ägyptisches Museum und Papyrussammlung, Staatliche Museen zu Berlin – Preußischer Kulturbesitz, Inv. ÄM 14145

THE SUN, MOON AND STARS – AN INTRODUCTION

Whether in the ancient Near East or among the ancient Egyptians, whether in early medieval and Christian Europe or among the cultures of the pre-Columbian Americas, Africa, Asia or Australia, deities were linked with the sun, moon and stars everywhere – or were viewed as divine signs in the heavens. They were venerated everywhere but also feared. After all, in the magical, mythological and religious conceptions prevailing in all those places and times, the heavenly

2 König Assur-nasirpal II. (reg. 883–859 v. Chr.) mit Helm, neuassyrisch, 883–859 v. Chr., Kalkstein.
King Assur-nasirpal II (reign 883–859 BC) wearing a helmet, Neo-Assyrian, limestone
The Fitzwilliam Museum, Cambridge, Inv. ANE.3.1942

3 Der Sonnengott Helios in Quadriga, Metope vom Nordostecksblock des Triglyphon des Athenatempels in Ilion/Troja, Türkei, 300–280 v. Chr., Marmor, H 85,5 cm, B 86,3 cm (Metope). The sun god Helios in a quadriga, metope from the north-east corner block of the triglyph in the Athena temple in Ilion/Troja, Turkey, 300–280 BC, marble, H 85.5, W 86.3 cm (metope). Antikensammlung, Staatliche Museen zu Berlin – Preußischer Kulturbesitz, Inv. LV 21,1 (LG)

bodies were regarded, on the one hand, as preservers of good fortune and prosperity, on the other, however, as harbingers of, and vehicles for, evil and the forces of evil.

From antiquity to the present day, poets, composers and painters have paid homage to the heavenly bodies. And artisans have invented exquisite things made of gold, silver, ivory and many other precious materials, objects with which they have represented and invoked the powers and forces of the heavenly bodies.

Ancient mythologies

The heavenly bodies have long had names. In ancient Egypt there was a sun god, Re, or Ra, who has come down to us in numerous representations. The moon god venerated by the ancient Egyptians was Iah, but Thoth, a deity with the head of an ibis, was also worshipped as a moon god and was even sometimes represented as a baboon with the crescent moon on his head (Fig. 5). In the fourteenth century BC the pharaoh Akhenaten created what was probably the earliest monotheistic religion, centred on the worship of Aten, or Aton, the disc of the sun (Fig. 1).

Shamash was the name of the solar deity venerated among the Assyrians and Babylonians. The primary deity of Babylon was later Marduk, who was also associated with the 'sea of the setting sun'. Sin was venerated as a moon god.

4   Mithras Tauroctonus, römisch, 2.–3. Jh. n. Chr., Marmor, 84,5 × 127,5 cm.
Mithras Tauroctonus, Roman, 2nd–3rd century AD, marble, 84.5 × 127.5 cm.
Courtesy of Rupert Wace Ancient Art, London

5 Statuette des ägyptischen Gottes Thot in Gestalt eines Pavians, Ägypten, ptolemäisch, 332–330 v. Chr., Fayence, Silber, Gold, 15 × 5 × 5,6 cm. Statuette of the Egyptian god Thoth as a baboon, Ptolemaic period, 332–330 BC, faience, silver, gold, 15 × 5 × 5.6 cm. Musée du Louvre, Paris, Département des Antiquités égyptiennes, Inv. E 17496

als Mondgottheit, im vorislamischen Arabien schließlich finden sich die Mondgötter Hubal, Tal'ab und Wadd.

Die Griechen kannten neben dem Lichtgott Apollon den Sonnengott Helios (Abb. 3) und widmeten ihm den sogenannten Koloss von Rhodos.[1] Selene, Danaë und Artemis wurden mit dem Mond in Zusammenhang gebracht. Die Römer nannten ihren Sonnengott Sol; zu ihm gesellte sich Mithras, dessen Kult seinen Ursprung zwar im Orient hatte, der aber – in veränderter Form – einen religiösen Siegeszug durch das ganze römische Reich antrat (Abb. 4). Als Mondgöttinnen wurden Luna und Diana verehrt (Abb. 6).

Im nördlichen Europa nannten die Kelten ihre Sonnengötter Lugh und Sulis, die slawischen Völker verehrten Svarožić, die Germanen Sunna und Sol. In skandinavischen Mythen findet sich zudem der Mondgott Mani.

Auch auf dem amerikanischen Kontinent wurden Sonnengottheiten angebetet: Die Inkakönige in Peru verehrten Inti, die Azteken in Mexiko die Sonnengötter Tonatiuh sowie Huitzilopochtli und dessen Mondschwester Coyolxauhqui. Noch heute legen die Sonnen- und die Mondpyramide in den Tempelanlagen von Teotihuacan beredtes Zeugnis von der Verehrung ab. Bei den Sioux in den nordamerikanischen Plains galt Wi als der die Sonne repräsentierende Gott. Die Inuit kannten Malina.

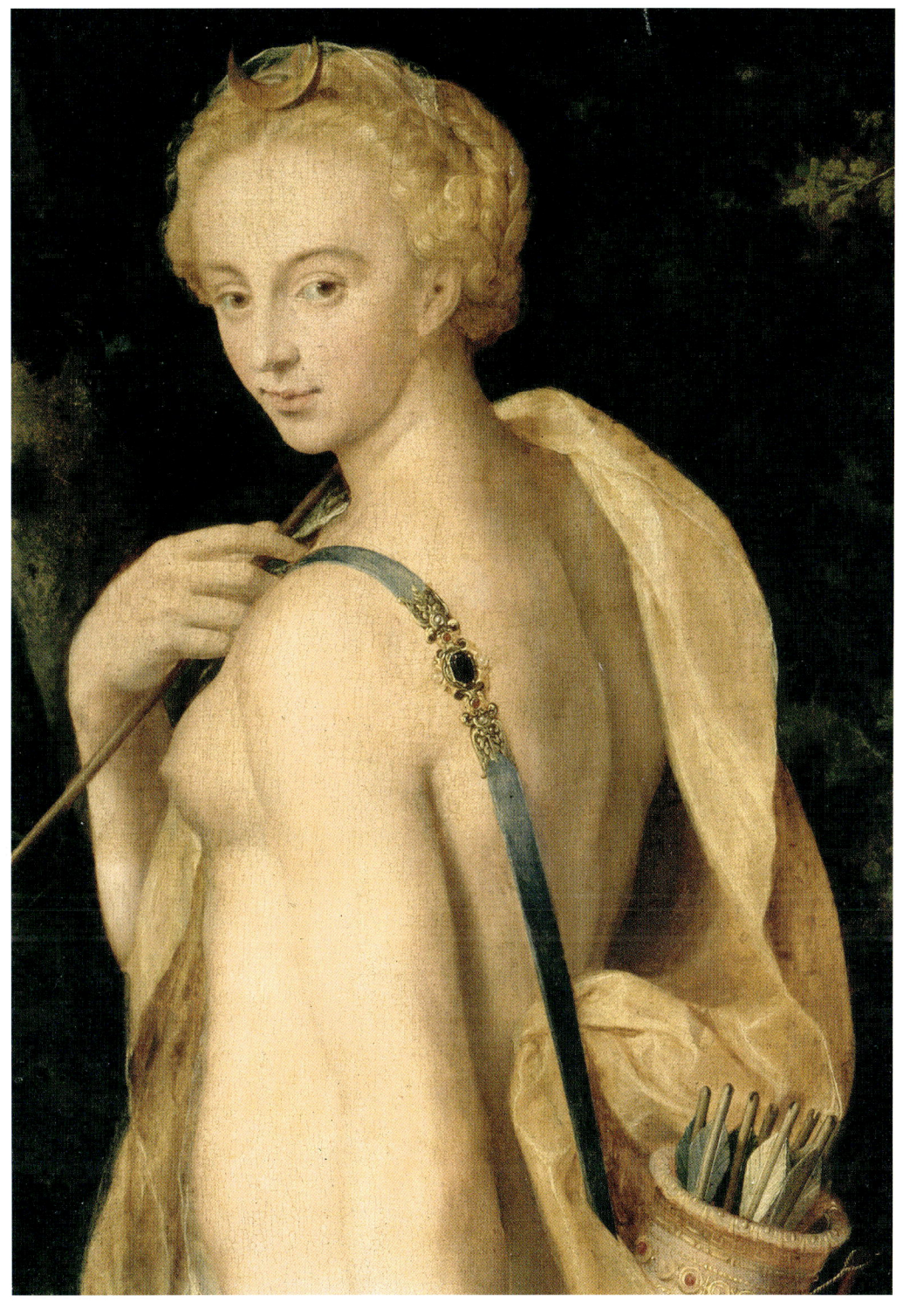

6 Schule von Fontainebleau, *Diana als Jägerin* (Detail), Mitte 16. Jh., Öl auf Leinwand, 191 × 132 cm. École de Fontainebleau, *Diane the Huntress* (detail), mid-16th century, oil on canvas, 191 × 132 cm. Musée du Louvre, Paris, Inv. INV445

7 Himmelsscheibe von Nebra, frühe Bronzezeit, um 1600 v. Chr., Bronze mit Goldauflagen, Dm ca. 32 cm. Nebra sky disc, early Bronze Age, c.1600 BC, bronze with gold inlay, dia. c.32 cm. Landesmuseum für Vorgeschichte, Halle (Saale)

Im Hinduismus ist Surya als Sonnengottheit bekannt, dort begegnet man auch dem Mondgott Chandra. Im Shintoismus schließlich wurde die Sonnengottheit Amaterasu und der Mondgott Tsukiyomi verehrt. In den großen Mythologien und Religionen waren somit die beiden mächtigen Himmelskörper mit magischen Funktionen ausgestattet.

Die aus irdischer Sicht eher „kleinen" Sterne und Planeten wurden in der griechischen und römischen Sagenwelt oft mit den Namen olympischer Götter belegt. Bis heute tragen die Planeten Namen römischer Gottheiten. Und auch immer noch gilt für viele Menschen die Aussage Ciceros: „Den Gestirnen ist Göttlichkeit zuzuerkennen".[2] So steht der Planet Jupiter – die oberste Gottheit der römischen Religion – unter anderem für Macht, Pracht und Glück, Venus – als Liebesgöttin – versinnbildlicht neben Liebe auch Schönheit und erotisches Verlangen und Mars – der Gott des Krieges – wird mit Kampf, Streit und Energie in Verbindung gebracht.[3]

Moreover, in Babylonian mythology there is a moon goddess called Annit. Utu – son of Nanna, the moon god – was venerated as a solar deity in Sumer. Arinna was the Hittite sun goddess. In Zoroastrian mythology, Mah, or Māonghah, appears as a moon deity. Finally, in pre-Islamic Arabia, Hubal, Tal'ab and Wadd were the moon deities.

The Greek sun god and god of light was Apollo, and Helios was the personification of the sun (Fig. 3). The celebrated Colossus of Rhodes was consecrated to Helios.[1] Selene, Danaë and Artemis were all associated with the moon in ancient Greece. The Romans named their sun god Sol. Mithras, whose cult originated in the East, was depicted in company with Sol. The Mithraic cult – in a changed form – swept triumphantly through the Roman Empire (Fig. 4). Roman deities venerated in association with the moon were Luna, the personification of the moon, and Diana, goddess of the moon (Fig. 6).

In northern Europe the Celts called their sun gods Lugh and Sulis. Slavic peoples venerated Svarožić while the Teutons worshipped Sunna and Sol. Scandinavian myths also have a moon good, Mani.

Solar deities were also worshipped in both South and North America: the Inca kings in Peru venerated Inti. The Aztecs in Mexico had two sun gods: Tonatiuh and Huitzilopochtli, and the latter's sister, Coyolxauhqui, was associated with the moon. The Sun and Moon Pyramids in the temple precincts at Teotihuacan bear eloquent witness to the scale on which these deities were worshipped. Among the Sioux on the North American plains, Wi was regarded as the deity representing the sun. The Inuit solar deity was called Malina.

Finally, in Hinduism the solar deity is known as Surya, and a lunar deity, Chandra, is also encountered in that religion. In Shintoism Amaterasu was venerated as the goddess of the sun and Tsukiyomi was the god of the moon. In the great mythologies and religions, therefore, magical functions were ascribed to the two most powerful heavenly bodies.

The stars and planets that tend to look 'small' to the naked eye as seen from Earth were often given the names of Olympian gods in Greek and Roman mythology. Even now the planets bear the names of Roman deities. And for many people Cicero's pronouncement still holds: 'Having thus ascertained the divinity of the universe, we must attribute the same quality to the heavenly bodies, which are created from the purist and most mobile portion of aether'.[2] The planet Jupiter – the supreme deity in the Roman pantheon – stands, among other things, for power, splendour and good fortune. Venus, as the goddess of love, symbolises – along with love – beauty and erotic yearnings. Mars, the god of war, is associated with battle, strife and energy.[3]

In many Indo-European languages, the names used for the days of the week still reveal the link with the heavenly bodies: this is quite obviously the case with *Sonntag* and *Montag* in German and Sunday, Monday, and Saturday (Saturn) in English. In French, as in other Romance languages, the names for the days of the week derive from the moon (luna: *lundi*), Mars (*mardi*), Mercury (*mercredi*) and Jupiter (*jeudi*).

Alongside the sun, moon and planets, the fixed stars also played a significant role in Greek mythology: as the story goes, the Seven Sisters, the Pleiades, were transformed into doves and ultimately transplanted to the sky as a cluster of seven stars. The Nebra sky disc (Fig. 7), a bronze disc with gold appliqués (which is presumed to date from about 1600 BC), is regarded as the earliest known

In vielen Sprachen lassen die Namen der Wochentage noch heute die Verbindung zu den Gestirnen erkennen: ganz offensichtlich bei Sonntag und Montag im Deutschen oder bei *Sunday*, *Monday* und *Saturday* (Saturn) im Englischen. Im Französischen – wie in anderen romanischen Sprachen – finden sich beispielsweise der Mond *(lundi)*, der Mars *(mardi)*, der Merkur *(mercredi)* und der Jupiter *(jeudi)* als Namenspatrone der Wochentage.

Neben Sonne, Mond und den Planeten spielten in der griechischen Mythologie aber auch die Fixsterne eine bedeutende Rolle: So wird etwa von sieben Schwestern berichtet, den Plejaden, die in Tauben verwandelt und schließlich als siebenteiliges Sternbild an den Himmel versetzt wurden. Die Himmelsscheibe von Nebra (Abb. 7), eine runde Platte aus Bronze mit Goldapplikationen (vermutlich aus der Zeit um 1600 v. Chr.), gilt als älteste Darstellung des Himmels überhaupt. Zwar stammt der bronzezeitliche Fund aus Mitteleuropa, weshalb kein direkter Bezug zur griechischen Mythologie gegeben ist. Dennoch geht die Wissenschaft davon aus, dass es sich bei der Gruppe von sieben Sternen, die auf der Scheibe zwischen der Sonne und der Mondsichel angeordnet sind, um die Plejaden handelt – ein Hinweis darauf, dass dem markanten Sternhaufen auch im nördlichen Europa magische Qualitäten zugesprochen wurden.

Judentum, Christentum und Islam

Als monotheistische Religionen kennen weder Juden- noch Christentum einen Sonnen- oder einen Mondgott. Ebenso wenig wird den Sternen eine göttliche Qualität zugesprochen. Und doch spielen im Alten wie im Neuen Testament die Gestirne immer wieder eine wichtige Rolle. Im ersten Buch Mose wird in der Schöpfungsgeschichte auf deren Bedeutung hingewiesen: „Und Gott machte zwei große Lichter: ein großes Licht, das den Tag regiere, und ein kleines Licht, das die Nacht regiere, dazu auch Sterne".[4] In den Psalmen wird Gott dafür gedankt, dass er die Gestirne geschaffen hat[5] und die Himmelskörper selbst werden aufgefordert: „Lobet ihn, Sonne und Mond; lobet ihn, alle leuchtenden Sterne".[6] Der alttestamentarische Herr Zebaoth wird im Psalm 84 folgendermaßen benannt: „Denn Gott der Herr ist Sonne und Schild",[7] wodurch auch hier indirekt Gott mit der Sonne gleichgesetzt wird.

Der Evangelist Matthäus berichtet vom „Stern von Bethlehem", den die Weisen aus dem Morgenlande gesehen hatten, und der sie zum Geburtsort dessen führte, der „über das Volk Israel ein Herr sei".[8] Viele altorientalische Mythen sprechen vom Stern als einem Symbol herrschaftlicher Macht, und so ist es nicht verwunderlich, dass der „Stern von Bethlehem" den neugeborenen „König der Juden" ankündigt.

In der Offenbarung des Johannes erfährt man außerdem von dem apokalyptischen Weib: „eine Frau, mit der Sonne bekleidet, und dem Mond unter ihren

representation of the night sky. This stunning Bronze Age find is from central Europe, which means it has no direct link to Greek mythology. Nonetheless, archaeologists assume that the seven stars which are arranged on the disc in a cluster between the sun and the crescent moon are the Pleiades – a hint that magical properties might have been imputed to the distinctive grouping of stars in northern Europe as well.

8   Albrecht Dürer, *Mondsichelmadonna*, 1499, Radierung, 10,8 × 7,7 cm, Privatsammlung. Albrecht Dürer, *The Virgin and Child on a Crescent*, 1499, engraving, 10.8 × 7.7 cm, private collection

9 Judenstern, Deutschland, nach 1941, Regeneratzellulose, bedruckt, Dm 9,5 cm. Jewish badge, Germany, after 1941, regenerated cellulose, printed, dia. 9.5 cm.
Deutsches Historisches Museum, Berlin, Inv. A 2002/2

Füßen und auf ihrem Haupt eine Krone von zwölf Sternen" (die die zwölf Stämme Israels bezeichnen).[9] Das apokalyptische Weib ist die Voraussetzung für die seit dem hohen Mittelalter, besonders aber im Barock so beliebte Darstellung Marias als „Mondsichelmadonna" (Abb. 8). Christus selbst wird in der Offenbarung mit den Worten zitiert: „Ich bin die Wurzel und der Stamm Davids, der strahlende Morgenstern".[10]

Auch in mehreren Suren des Koran wird auf die Sonne, den Mond und die Sterne hingewiesen, ohne dass göttliche Funktionen mit den Gestirnen verbunden sind. Es wird allerdings mehrfach betont, dass Allah „die Sonne und den Mond und die Sterne, seinem Gesetz dienstbar" geschaffen hat.[11]

Heraldik und politische Symbole

Die Mondsichel als das Zeichen des Islam lässt sich möglicherweise auf vorislamisch-arabische Vorstellungen zurückführen, hat aber keine im eigentlichen Sinne religiöse Bedeutung. In der heutigen islamischen Welt weist der Halbmond als zunehmender Mond in erster Linie auf eine politische Identität hin, was sich in der Heraldik und in den Nationalflaggen vieler islamischer Länder niederschlägt (vgl. auch S. 94). Der Rote Halbmond ist in islamischen Ländern daher auch das Symbol für Hilfsorganisationen, die dem Roten Kreuz entsprechen. In Israel wurde für die gleiche Funktion ein roter Sechsstern gewählt, der als *Magen David Adom* (Roter Schild Davids) bezeichnet wird.

Judaism, Christianity and Islam

As monotheistic religions, Judaism and Christianity do not have sun or moon gods. Nor are divine qualities attributed to the stars. Nonetheless the heavenly bodies frequently play an important role in both the Old Testament and the New Testament. Their importance is referred to in the story of the Creation in the first book of Genesis: 'And God then made two great lights: the greater light to rule the day, and the lesse light to rule the night: he made also the starres'.[4] In the Psalms God is thanked for having made the stars,[5] and the heavenly bodies themselves are exhorted: 'Praise ye him Sunne and moone: praise him all ye starres of light'.[6] Jehovah, the Old Testament God of Israel, is described as follows in Psalm 84: 'For the Lord God is a sunne and shield', thus equated metaphorically with the sun here as well.[7]

Matthew the Evangelist reports of a 'starre in the East', which the kings from the orient had seen and which led them to the birthplace of him who is 'the King of the Jewes that is borne'.[8] Since many Near Eastern myths speak of the star as a symbol of royal power, it is not surprising that the 'Star of Bethlehem' proclaims the birth of the newborn 'King of the Jewes'.

In the Revelation of Saint John the Divine, we also learn of the Woman of the Apocalypse: 'A woman clothed with the sunne, and the moone was under her feete, and upon her head a crowne of twelve starres': the twelve stars represent the twelve tribes of Israel.[9] Since the high Middle Ages, and later in the Baroque era especially, the Woman of the Apocalypse had been the archetype for the Virgin represented as a 'Madonna on the Crescent Moon' (Fig. 8). Christ himself is quoted in Revelation as saying: 'I am the roote and the generation of David, and the brightest morning starre'.[10]

Several Qur'an suras refer to the sun, moon and stars, without associating divine functions with the heavenly bodies. However, it is emphasised several times that Allah created 'the sun, moon and the stars, subjected by His command'.[11]

Heraldry and political symbols

The crescent moon as the sign of Islam may possibly go back to pre-Islamic Arab ideas but it does not have religious significance in the strict sense of the term. In the Islamic world today the half moon, as a waxing moon, chiefly refers to a political identity that is reflected in the heraldry and national flags of many Islamic countries (see also p. 89). The Red Crescent is the symbol in Islamic countries for relief organisations corresponding to the Red Cross. In Israel a red six-pointed star, which is called Magen David Adom (Red Shield of David), was chosen for the same function.

The star, as Magen David, plays an important role in Judaism. A blue, six-pointed star on a white ground adorns the flag of the state of Israel. The so-called *Judenstern* [Jew star], on the other hand, was abused during the Third Reich as a demeaning sign that outlawed the wearer from society. In National Socialist Germany and countries occupied by Germany this yellow six-pointed star was employed as a badge to identify people classified by the authorities as 'of Jewish descent' (Fig. 9).

The swastika underwent similar reinterpretation at the same time. It had found its way via India and China to Japan, Land of the Rising Sun, as a sun symbol. And in Europe, too, the swastika had been in use since prehistorical times – for instance, as a variant of the fret on vases from Minoan Crete. The

10 Die Flagge Brasiliens.
The Brazilian flag

Generell spielt der Stern als *Magen David* im Judentum eine wichtige Rolle. So schmückt der blaue sechsstrahlige Stern auf weißem Grund die Flagge des Staates Israel. Als herabwürdigendes und den Träger ausgrenzendes Zeichen hingegen wurde der sogenannte „Judenstern" während des Dritten Reiches missbraucht. Im nationalsozialistischen Deutschland und in den von Deutschland besetzten Ländern diente er zur Kennzeichnung von Menschen jüdischer Abstammung (Abb. 9).

Eine ähnliche Umdeutung erfuhr in dieser Zeit die Swastika. Als Sonnensymbol hatte sie von Indien über China nach Japan, dem Land der aufgehenden Sonne, ihren Weg gefunden. Und auch in Europa war die Swastika seit frühgeschichtlicher Zeit in Gebrauch, etwa als Abwandlungen von Mäandern auf minoischen Vasen. Der Missbrauch als „Hakenkreuz" durch die deutschen Nationalsozialisten macht es allerdings heute schwierig, in dem Zeichen noch einen Bezug zur Sonne zu erkennen.

Dennoch besitzen die Gestirne selbst nach wie vor einen großen Symbolwert im Bereich der Heraldik. Von den zurzeit 193 Mitgliedstaaten der Vereinten Nationen (Stand 2014) führen fast die Hälfte entweder Sonne, Mond oder Sterne – oft auch eine Kombination von ihnen – in ihren Wappen und auf ihren Fahnen. Bemerkenswert ist die Flagge Brasiliens, in der die 27 Sterne für die 26 Bundesstaaten sowie den Bundesdistrikt stehen – und zwar entsprechend ihrer Konstellation über Rio de Janeiro am 15. November 1889, als die Republik Brasilien proklamiert wurde (Abb. 10).

Die 50 Sterne in der Flagge der Vereinigten Staaten von Amerika, dem sogenannten „Sternenbanner", symbolisieren ebenfalls die Bundesstaaten der USA.

abuse of the swastika motif as the *Hakenkreuz* [hooked cross] by the German National Socialists has, however, made it difficult to recognise any reference to the sun in this sign nowadays.

Nevertheless, the heavenly bodies have retained enormous symbolic value in the field of heraldry. Of the 193 countries that are currently (as of 2014) members of the United Nations, nearly half display the sun, moon or stars – often a combination of them – in their coats of arms and national seals and on their flags. A remarkable example is the Brazilian flag, which features twenty-seven stars standing for twenty-six federal states and one federal district containing the capital city – even matching their position in the sky above Rio de Janeiro on 15 November 1889, when Brazil was proclaimed a republic (Fig. 10).

The fifty stars on the flag, known as the 'star-spangled banner', of the United States of America also symbolise the individual federal states of this federal republic. The emblem of the European Union, on the other hand, bears twelve five-pointed stars forming a circle, which do not correspond to the number of member states. And the logo of the European Central Bank (ECB) features a euro sign encircled by the twelve stars representing the European Union.

Cities, including Halle an der Saale and Worms in Germany, Maastricht in the Netherlands, Portsmouth in England and Portsmouth, Rhode Island, in the United States, also have stars in their coats of arms. This is also true of such regions and administrative units as the Australian state of Victoria and the Swiss canton of Valais.

The five-pointed red star is the symbol of the Socialist and Communist world view. Closely linked with the 1917 October Revolution in Russia, it was part of the coat of arms and the flag of the former Soviet Union. The German far-left militant organisation that operated as a terrorist group in the Federal Republic of Germany in the 1970s, the Rote Armee Fraktion [Red Army Faction], also identified with the red-star symbol, combining it with a black submachine gun overlaid with the letters RAF in white. Still, not all uses to which the red star has been put are so menacing: some European football clubs, such as Red Star Belgrade and Roter Stern Leipzig, which was only founded in 1999, boast the red star in their names and their logo.

Distinction

Stars have often served as a means and sign of distinction. The star to be worn on the breast awarded by many civil and military orders emphatically testifies to this (Fig. 12). One such order that became very well known was the Order of the Red Star, established in 1930 and a much coveted distinction in the former USSR. The sheriff's star-shaped badge in the United States, Canada and Australia is both a badge and identifying emblem of officials entrusted with law enforcement.

Aside from four-star generals in the military, in civilian life stars also stand for status and fame, with three-star restaurants and five-star hotels. And not least, there is the Hollywood Walk of Fame on Hollywood Boulevard and Vine Street in Los Angeles. Here stars and starlets from cinema, music, show business and beyond are honoured for their achievements in the entertainment industry by metal and terrazzo stars set into the pavement. Marilyn Monroe (Fig. 11) is represented here and so are Peter Falk, Janis Joplin and – since 2015 – Snoopy from *Peanuts*.

Das Emblem der Europäischen Union hingegen trägt zwölf fünfstrahlige Sterne, die einen Kreis bilden und von der Zahl der Mitgliedsstaaten unabhängig sind. Im Logo der Europäischen Zentralbank (EZB) wird ein Euro-Zeichen von den zwölf Sternen umrahmt.

Auch Städte wie beispielsweise Halle an der Saale und Worms in Deutschland oder Maastricht in den Niederlanden, Portsmouth in England und Portsmouth in Rhode Island (USA) haben Gestirne in ihren Wappen. Ebenso verschiedene Regionen und Länder wie der australische Bundesstaat Victoria und der Schweizer Kanton Wallis.

Der fünfzackige Rote Stern gilt als Symbol für die sozialistische bzw. kommunistische Weltanschauung. Er ist eng mit der russischen Oktoberrevolution von 1917 verbunden und war Teil des Wappens und der Flagge der Sowjetunion. Auch die deutsche linksextremistische Terrorvereinigung der 1970er-Jahre, die Rote Armee Fraktion, identifizierte sich mit dem Symbol und verband es mit einem schwarzen Maschinengewehr, vor das die Buchstaben RAF gelegt wurden. Doch nicht alle Einsatzfelder des Roten Sterns sind so bedrohlich: Einige Fußballvereine wie zum Beispiel „Roter Stern Belgrad" oder der erst 1999 gegründete Club „Roter Stern Leipzig" tragen den Stern im Namen und im Logo.

11 Marilyn Monroes Stern auf dem Hollywood Walk of Fame, 1960. Marilyn Monroe's star on the Hollywood Walk of Fame, 1960

Auszeichnung Sterne dienten und dienen häufig als Mittel und Zeichen der Auszeichnung. Die Bruststerne vieler ziviler und militärischer Orden stellen dies nachdrücklich unter Beweis (Abb. 12). Besonders bekannt geworden ist der 1930 gestiftete „Rote Stern", eine begehrte Auszeichnung in der ehemaligen UdSSR. Der Sheriffstern in den Vereinigten Staaten von Amerika, in Kanada und in Australien ist Abzeichen und Kennzeichen der mit polizeilichen Aufgaben betrauten Amtspersonen.

12 Christian Friedrich Reinhold Lisiewsky, *Friedrich II. der Große mit dem Orden vom Schwarzen Adler*, 1782, Öl auf Leinwand, 66,5 × 52,5 cm. Christian Friedrich Reinhold Lisiewsky, *Friedrich II (the Great) with Order of the Black Eagle*, 1782, oil on canvas, 66.5 × 52.5 cm. Nationalgalerie, Staatliche Museen zu Berlin – Preußischer Kulturbesitz, Inv. A II 919

In sports stars also play an important role in the form of achievement awards. Every year the German Olympic Sports Confederation awards *Sterne des Sports* [Sports Stars] jointly with a banking group to promote popular sports. And the German national football team earned a fourth star in Brazil in 2014 for winning the FIFA World Cup four times. The official logo of the UEFA Champions League games and the ball itself are respectively composed of, and decorated with, stars.

Auch im zivilen Bereich stehen Sterne für Rang und Ruhm: So gibt es nicht nur Vier-Sterne-Generäle, sondern auch Drei-Sterne-Restaurants und Fünf-Sterne-Hotels. Und nicht zuletzt gibt es den *Walk of Fame* auf dem Hollywood Boulevard in Los Angeles. Hier werden Stars und Sternchen aus Film, Musik und Showgeschäft mit im Boden eingelassenen Metallsternen geehrt. Marilyn Monroe (Abb. 11) ist hier ebenso vertreten wie Peter Falk, Janis Joplin und – seit 2015 – Snoopy von den Peanuts.

Im Sport spielen Sterne bei Ehrungen ebenfalls eine wichtige Rolle. Vom Deutschen Olympischen Sportbund werden zusammen mit einer Bankengruppe alljährlich die *Sterne des Sports* zur Förderung des Breitensports verliehen. Und die deutsche Fußball-Nationalmannschaft hat sich 2014 in Brasilien einen vierten Stern für die viermalige Meisterschaft im World Cup erkämpft. Das offizielle Logo der Champions League-Spiele und der Ball selbst sind mit Sternen geschmückt.

Mit dem dreizackigen Mercedes-Stern mag sich manch ein Autobesitzer selbst schmückend auszeichnen. Und wenn er gerade nicht mit seinem Wagen unterwegs ist, sorgt ein in Kooperation mit Swarovski luxuriös aufgewerteter elektronischer Schlüssel mit zentralem Stern und glitzernden Kristallen an den Seiten für Aufsehen. Auch andere Automarken zieren sich mit dem Sternsymbol: Das Logo des amerikanischen Herstellers Chrysler besteht aus einem Stern mit fünf Strahlen, der japanische Autobauer Subaru hingegen trägt sechs Sterne in seinem Markenzeichen.

Bildende Kunst

Seit Jahrtausenden spielten und spielen die Gestirne eine wichtige Rolle in der bildenden Kunst – in den altorientalischen Kulturen ebenso wie in der klassischen Antike, dem Mittelalter und der Neuzeit. Der Maler Caspar David Friedrich sei mit seinen berühmten Sonnenauf- und -untergängen als Repräsentant des 19. Jahrhunderts besonders in Erinnerung gerufen.

In der frühen Moderne ist es vor allem Vincent van Gogh, der Sonne, Mond und Sternen huldigt (Abb. 13). Joan Mirós *Rote Sonnen* glühen in leidenschaftlichem Feuer und Jean Lurçat beschäftigte sich nicht nur auf Tapisserien und in keramischen Arbeiten mit den Zeichen des Himmels, er hat auch Schmuckstücke mit Titeln wie *Sonne* und *Mond* entworfen (s. Abb. 108).

Im Garten des Museums der schweizerischen Stadt Freiburg steht die farbige Skulptur *La Grande Lune* von Niki de Saint Phalle, und vor dem Badischen Staatstheater in Karlsruhe sind die Skulpturen *Sonne* und *Mond* von Markus Lüpertz aus dem Jahr 1989 aufgestellt. Der Licht- und ZERO-Künstler Otto Piene hat sich in seinen *Sky Events* auf beeindruckende Weise mit den Gestirnen auseinandergesetzt, und auch in den Lichtkunstarbeiten von Olafur Eliasson spielen die Himmelskörper eine wichtige Rolle.

13   Vincent van Gogh, *Sternennacht,* Saint-Rémy, 1889, Öl auf Leinwand, 73,7 × 92,1 cm. Vincent van Gogh, *The Starry Night*, Saint-Rémy, 1889, oil on canvas, 73.7 × 92.1 cm. Museum of Modern Art, New York, Inv. 472.1941

Many proud car owners award themselves a distinction with the three-pointed star on their Mercedes. And when they aren't actually driving it, electronic keys dangling from an officially licensed key chain sumptuously embellished with a central star surrounded by a ring of glittering crystals courtesy of Swarovski are an eye-catching status symbol. Other lesser marques sport starry symbols: the logo of the American car manufacturer Chrysler consists of a five-pointed star while the emblem of the Japanese car manufacturer Subaru is composed of six stars.

Fine art
For thousands of years the heavenly bodies have played an important role in fine art – in Near Eastern civilisations, classical antiquity, the Middle Ages and the Modern age. The painter Caspar David Friedrich with his celebrated sunsets and sunrises is particularly memorable as a representative of the nineteenth century.

14 Karl Friedrich Schinkel, *Die Sternenhalle der Königin der Nacht*, Bühnenbildentwurf für die Oper *Die Zauberflöte* von Wolfgang Amadeus Mozart, um 1815, Gouache, handgeschöpftes Papier, 46,4 × 61,5 cm. Karl Friedrich Schinkel, *Hall of Stars* representing the Queen of the Night, stage design for Wolfgang Amadeus Mozart's *The Magic Flute*, c. 1815, gouache, handmade paper, 46.4 × 61.5 cm. Kupferstichkabinett, Staatliche Museen zu Berlin – Preußischer Kulturbesitz, Inv. SM 22c.121

Bühnenbild   Berühmt wurde Karl Friedrich Schinkels Bühnenbild für Mozarts *Zauberflöte* von 1815. Im Finale des zweiten Aktes erscheint die Königin der Nacht wie eine Mondsichelmadonna vor breitem Sternenhimmel (Abb. 14), während Sarastro die Arie *Die Strahlen der Sonne vertreiben die Nacht* singt. Der englische Schmuckkünstler Kevin Coates hat das Thema in seinem Kopfschmuck *Entry of the Queen of the Night* von 1996 eindrucksvoll aufgenommen (s. Abb. 117), und auch David Watkins nennt eine Brosche von 1998 *Königin der Nacht*.

Verwandt mit Schinkels Bühnenbild sind einige Arbeiten des Illustrators, Bühnenbildners und Modedesigners Erté, der unter anderem für Filme und Revuen aufwändige Ausstattungen entworfen hat. Und auch die Kuppeln der von Wassili

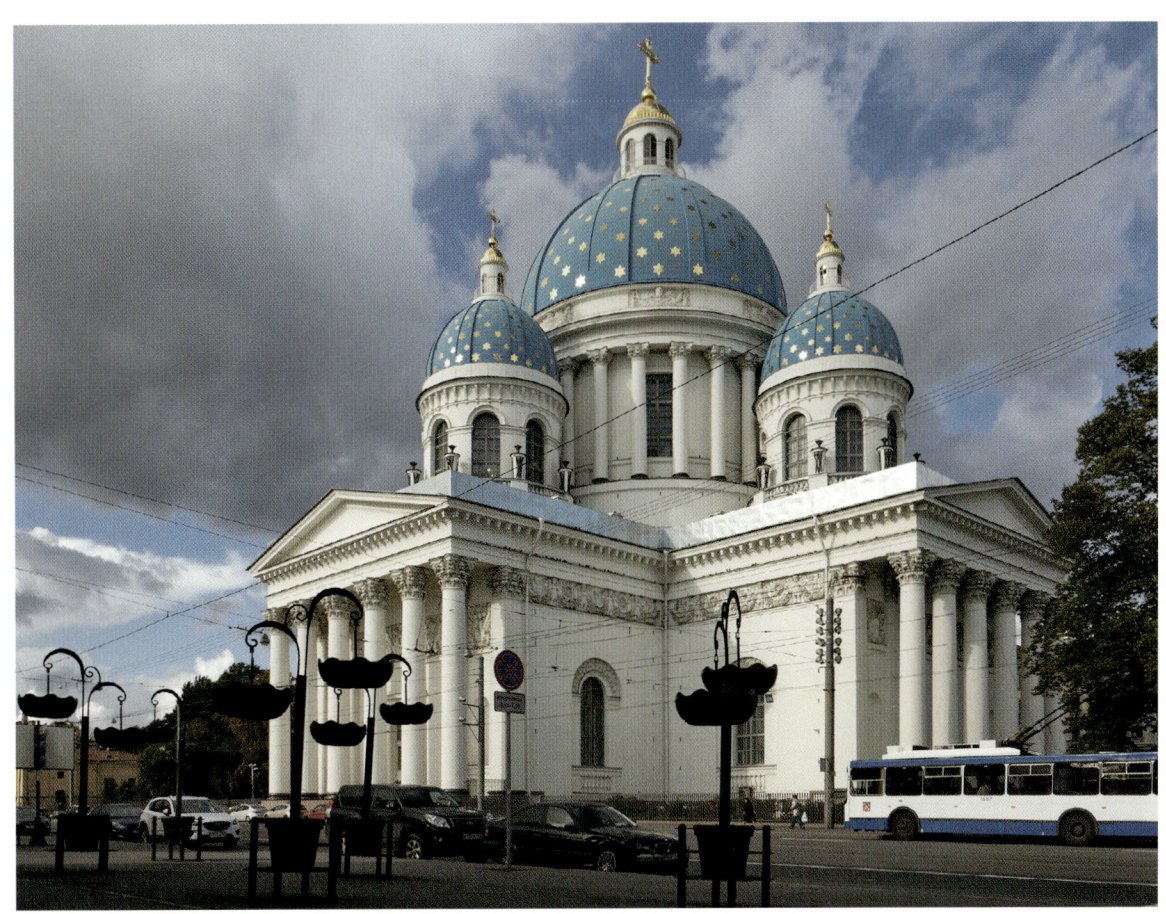

15 Dreifaltigkeitskathedrale, St. Petersburg, 1828–1835 nach Plänen von Wassili Petrowitsch Stassow errichtet. Trinity Cathedral, St Petersburg, carried out in 1828–1835 after plans by Vasily Petrovich Stasov

Among the early Moderns, Vincent van Gogh most notably pays tribute to the sun, moon and stars (Fig. 13). Joan Miró's *Red Suns* glow with ardent fire. And Jean Lurçat investigated the celestial bodies not only on Aubusson tapestries and ceramics but also designed pieces of jewellery with titles such as *Sun* and *Moon* (see Fig. 108).

The colourful Niki de Saint Phalle sculpture *La Grande Lune* [*Big Moon*] stands in the garden of the Museum of Art and History in Fribourg, Switzerland. *Sonne* [*Sun*] and *Mond* [*Moon*] (1989) are sculptures by Markus Lüpertz that have been set up in front of the Badisches Staatstheater in Karlsruhe. Otto Piene, a co-founder of ZERO and a light artist, explored the heavenly bodies theme to impressive effect in his *Sky Events*. The heavenly bodies also play an important role in Olafur Eliasson's artworks in light.

Petrowitsch Stassow zwischen 1828 und 1835 erbauten Dreifaltigkeitskathedrale in Sankt Petersburg zeigen – ähnlich wie die Schinkelsche Bühnendekoration – das mit goldenen Sternen überzogene Firmament (Abb. 15).

Musik
Vielfältig sind die musikalischen Ausdrucksformen, in denen die Gestirne in Erscheinung treten. Mit den Worten „Weißt du, wieviel Sternlein stehen, an dem blauen Himmelszelt" beginnt eines der beliebtesten deutschen Wiegenlieder – es ist in der ersten Hälfte des 19. Jahrhunderts entstanden.

1851 schrieb Karl Enslin den Text zu dem Volkslied *Guter Mond, du gehst so stille*. Und das Gedicht *Der Mond ist aufgegangen* von Matthias Claudius wurde von Michael Haydn, Franz Schubert, Carl Orff und auch von Herbert Grönemeyer vertont. Der berühmte Bruder von Michael, Joseph Haydn, hat zudem die Oper *Il Mondo della Luna* komponiert. Beethovens *Mondscheinsonate*, die 1801 vollendet wurde, ist weltberühmt, sollte aber nicht mit Glenn Millers *Moonlight Serenade* aus dem Jahr 1939 verwechselt werden.

Nach einem Gedicht von Paul Verlaine veröffentlichte Claude Debussy im Jahre 1905 *Claire de Lune* als dritten Satz seiner *Suite bergamasque*. Die Operette *Frau Luna* von Paul Lincke, in der die Schlösser im Monde liegen, wurde 1922 in Berlin uraufgeführt, und in einem Film mit Heinz Rühmann aus dem Jahre 1955 heißt es „La le lu – nur der Mann im Mond schaut zu". Auch der moderne Komponist Edgar Rupp hat *Sechs Mondlieder* geschaffen. Und im Jahre 2006 choreographierte Pina Bausch ihr *Vollmond-Ballett*, bei dem die Liebe im Mittelpunkt steht.

Das Bach-Werke-Verzeichnis (BWV 1) nennt die Kantate *Wie schön leuchtet der Morgenstern*. Der Abendstern hingegen wird im dritten Akt von Richard Wagners *Tannhäuser* besungen: Wolfram von Eschenbach bezeichnet ihn dort als den lieblichsten aller Sterne. In Puccinis Oper *Tosca* heißt es in Bezug auf den nächtlichen Sternenhimmel insgesamt: „Und es blitzten die Sterne" (*E lucevan le stelle*).

Der Komponist und Autor Peter Schindler hat in seiner szenischen Kantate in zwei Akten *Sonne, Mond und Sterne* Gedichte und Texte aus vielen Jahrhunderten vertont: „Die Gedichte", so ist bei ihm nachzulesen, „handeln von den Himmelskörpern Sonne, Mond und Sterne; von Liebe, Sehnsucht, Leidenschaft, Zeit, Lebenskreislauf, von Träumen und vom Sterben."[12] Sie zeigen, bezogen auf die Gestirne und die ganze Welt, ein unendlich reiches Abbild von der Fülle menschlichen Lebens.

Die Sonne findet sich in Kirchenliedern wie *Die Güldne Sonne, voll Freud und Wonne* von Paul Gerhardt. Die Morgenstimmung im Moment der aufgehenden Sonne wird in der *Peer Gynt Suite Nr. 1* von Edvard Grieg zum musikalischen Erlebnis. Noch bekannter aber ist das neapolitanische Volkslied *O Sole Mio*. Es wurde

Stage design

The stage sets Karl Friedrich Schinkel designed for Mozart's *Magic Flute* in 1815 are famous. In the final scene of Act II, the Queen of the Night appears like a Madonna on the Crescent Moon against a broad starry sky (Fig. 14) as Sarastro sings the aria 'The Sun's Rays Drive Out the Night'. The English art jewellery maker Kevin Coates has memorably taken up the theme in *Entry of the Queen of the Night* (1996), a tiara (see Fig. 117), while David Watkins called a 1998 brooch *Queen of the Night*.

Some works by the illustrator, stage-set designer and fashion designer Erté, who designed elaborate sets for films and variety shows, are related to the Schinkel stage set. And even the blue domes of Trinity Cathedral in Saint Petersburg, built from 1828 to 1835 and designed by the architect Vasily Petrovich Stasov, represent the firmament dotted with golden stars – similar to the Schinkel stage set (Fig. 15).

Music

The heavenly bodies appear in manifold forms of expression in music. One of the most popular German lullabies – composed in the first half of the nineteenth century – begins with the words 'Weißt du, wieviel Sternlein stehen, an dem blauen Himmelszelt' ['Do you know how many little stars are set in heaven's blue tent'].

In 1851 Karl Enslin wrote the text of the folk song 'Guter Mond, du gehst so stille' ['Good Moon, You Go So Quietly']. The poem 'Der Mond ist aufgegangen' ['The Moon Has Risen'] by Matthias Claudius has been set to music by Michael Haydn, Franz Schubert, Carl Orff and even the German singer-songwriter Herbert Grönemeyer. Joseph Hayden, Michael Haydn's more famous brother, also composed an opera buffa about the moon: *Il Mondo della Luna* [*The World on the Moon*]. Finished in 1801, Beethoven's 'Mondscheinsonate' ['Moonlight Sonata'] is world famous but nonetheless should not be confused with Glenn Miller's 1939 'Moonlight Serenade'.

In 1905 Claude Debussy published 'Claire de Lune', after a poem by Paul Verlaine, as the third movement of his *Suite bergamasque*. *Frau Luna*, an operetta by Paul Lincke featuring castles on the moon, premiered in Berlin in 1922. A 1955 Heinz Rühmann film contains the line 'La le lu – nur der Mann im Mond schaut zu' ['La le lu – only the Man in the Moon is looking at you']. The modern composer Edgar Rupp wrote 'Sechs Mondlieder' ['Six Moon Songs']. And in 2006 Pina Bausch choreographed her *Vollmond-Ballet* [*Full-Moon Ballet*], which is about love.

J. S. Bach's Complete Works (BWV 1) lists a cantata under the title 'Wie schön leuchtet der Morgenstern' ['How Beautifully Shines the Morning Star']. The Evening Star, on the other hand, is praised in the third act of Wagner's *Tannhäuser*, in which Wolfram von Eschenbach calls it the loveliest of all stars. In the Puccini opera *Tosca* the starry night sky is evoked: 'E lucevan le stelle' ['And the stars were shining'].

Peter Schindler, writer and composer, has set to music poems and texts from several centuries in a scenic cantata in two acts, *Sonne, Mond und Sterne* [*Sun, Moon and Stars*]: 'The poems', he writes, 'are about the heavenly bodies, the sun, moon and stars; about love, yearning, passion, time, the life cycle, dreams and death.'[12] Referring to the heavenly bodies and the whole world, they reflect the infinite richness of human life.

von so berühmten Tenören wie Enrico Caruso, Beniamino Gigli, Mario Lanza, den Drei Tenören und von so manchem Schlagersänger interpretiert.

Überhaupt sind Schlager, Chansons und Evergreens voller Bezüge zu den Gestirnen: In einem unter anderem von Vico Torriani und Max Raabe gesungenen Klassiker von Gerhard Winkler erfährt man, was geschieht, „wenn bei Capri die rote Sonne im Meer versinkt, und am Himmel die bleiche Sichel des Mondes blinkt". Richard Rodgers schrieb 1933 *Blue Moon*, einen Song, der sich in der Folgezeit zu einem berühmten Evergreen entwickeln sollte.

Für den 1961 entstandenen Film *Frühstück bei Tiffany* vertonte Henry Mancini den Text des Hits *Moon River* von Johnny Mercer. Er wurde von Audrey Hepburn, Frank Sinatra, Rita Hayworth, Louis Armstrong, aber auch von Elton John interpretiert. Mit *Fly me to the Moon* landete Frank Sinatra einen weiteren Evergreen zum Thema Mond. Und Dean Martin ist überzeugt: „When the moon hits your eye like a big pizza pie, that's amore".

Caterina Valente verbindet die Gestirne mit Hoffnung und Freiheit, wenn sie singt: „Wo meine Sonne scheint und wo meine Sterne steh'n. Da kann man der Hoffnung Glanz und der Freiheit Licht in der Ferne seh'n." Und auch Dalida singt in den 1960er-Jahren ein Chanson, in dem sie die Sonne beschwört – es trägt den Titel *Soleil, Soleil*.

Pop- und Rockgruppen wie Die Prinzen und Rammstein wissen ebenfalls von dem Mann im Mond, von der Sonne und dem Morgenstern zu berichten. Das erfolgreichste Album von Pink Floyd trägt den Titel *The Dark Side of the Moon*. Al Jarreau singt von *Moonlighting*, Mike Oldfield vom *Moonlight Shadow* und die Heavy-Metal-Legende Ozzy Osborne von der *Bark at the Moon*. David Bowies letztes Album schließlich, das nur wenige Tage vor seinem Tod veröffentlicht wurde, trägt den Titel *Black Star*.

Literatur

Schon im Prolog des ersten Teils von Goethes *Faust* erscheint das Sonnenmotiv; dort heißt es: „Die Sonne tönt, nach alter Weise,/ In Brudersphären Wettgesang,/ und ihre vorgeschriebene Reise/ Vollendet sie mit Donnergang." Im zweiten Teil des *Faust* stellt der Astrologe eine Verbindung her zwischen der Sonne und dem Gold, wenn er sagt: „Die Sonne selbst, sie ist ein lautres Gold". Der Seher erwähnt auch „die keusche Luna" und verbindet somit den Mond mit dem Silber. Schließlich fasst der Astrologe zusammen: „Ja! wenn zu Sol sich Luna fein gesellt,/ Zum Silber Gold, dann ist es heitre Welt".[13]

Was Goethe im *Faust* den Astrologen sagen lässt, ist Gemeingut in den verschiedensten Gegenden der Welt. „Gold ist warm und hat etwas von der Sonne", sagt die heilige Kirchengelehrte Hildegard von Bingen im 12. Jahrhundert.[14] Und in allen Kulturen gibt es Märchen, die die Sonne, den Mond und die Sterne symbolhaft

The sun features in hymns, such as 'Die Güldne Sonne, voll Freud und Wonne' ['The Golden Sun, Full of Joy and Bliss'], EG 449 in the German Protestant hymnal, by the seventeenth-century German theologian Paul Gerhardt. The morning mood caught at sunrise in Edvard Grieg's *Peer Gynt Suite No. 1* is a musical event. More widely known is the Neapolitan folk song 'O Sole Mio' ['Sun of Mine']. It has been interpreted by such celebrated tenors as Enrico Caruso, Beniamino Gigli, Mario Lanza, the Three Tenors and many a pop singer.

Pop hits, chansons and evergreens are in fact full to bursting with allusions to the heavenly bodies: in a Gerhard Winkler (1906–1977) classic interpreted by, among others, Vico Torriani and Max Raabe listeners find out what happens, 'when at Capri the red sun sinks into the sea, and in the sky the pale sickle of the moon twinkles'. In 1933 Richard Rodgers wrote 'Blue Moon', a song that would fulfil its promise to become an evergreen everyone knows.

Henry Mancini set to music the Johnny Mercer lyrics 'Moon River' for the 1961 romantic comedy film *Breakfast at Tiffany's*. The song became a universal hit, interpreted variously by Audrey Hepburn, Frank Sinatra, Rita Hayworth, Louis Armstrong and, most recently, Elton John. With 'Fly me to the Moon' Frank Sinatra added another evergreen on the moon theme. And Dean Martin was convinced: 'When the moon hits your eye like a big pizza pie, that's amore'.

Caterina Valente associated the heavenly bodies with hope and freedom when she sang, 'Wo meine Sonne scheint und wo meine Sterne steh'n. Da kann man der Hoffnung Glanz und der Freiheit Licht in der Ferne seh'n.' ['Where my sun shines and where my stars stand. There you can see the brightness of hope and the light of freedom far away.'] And Dalida sang a chanson in the 1960s in which she invoked the sun – 'Soleil, Soleil' ['Sun, Sun'] was its title.

Pop and rock groups such as Die Prinzen and Rammstein have also had plenty to say about the Man in the Moon, the sun and the Morning Star. *The Dark Side of the Moon* was Pink Floyd's most successful album. In the 1980s Al Jarreau sang about 'Moonlighting' (1984), Mike Oldfield invoked 'Moonlight Shadow' (1983) and heavy-metal legend Ozzy Osborne's *Bark at the Moon* album was released in 1983. David Bowie's last album, released only a few days before he died, is *Black Star*.

Literature

The sun motif makes its appearance in Goethe's *Faust*, Part I, in the 'Prologue in Heaven', where it says, 'The Sun sings out, in ancient mode, / His note among his brother-spheres, / And ends his pre-determined road, / With peals of thunder for our ears.' In *Faust*, Part II, the Astrologer says, 'The Sun, himself, he is of purest gold'. The seer also mentions 'The chaste Moon's mood' and links the moon with silver, saying, 'Yes! When Sun and Moon are conjoined fine, / Silver and gold will make the whole world shine'.[13]

What Goethe has the Astrologer say in *Faust II* is a commonplace in many parts of the world. 'Gold is warm and has something of the Sun' according to the learned Saint Hildegard of Bingen in the twelfth century.[14] And in all cultures there are fairy tales about the sun, moon and stars, either on the symbolical plane or as real heavenly bodies. In Germany, for instance, in the Brothers Grimm. The best known of those tales are probably *Sterntaler* [*Star Money*] (Fig. 16) and *Allerleirauh* [*All-Kinds-of-Fur*]. Here the titular heroine owns three dresses, 'one as golden as the sun, one as silver as the moon and one as dazzling as the stars'.

oder als reale Himmelskörper zum Inhalt haben. In Deutschland zum Beispiel bei den Brüdern Grimm. Die bekanntesten sind wohl *Sterntaler* (Abb. 16) und *Allerleirauh*. Hier besitzt die Titelgestalt drei Kleider, „eins so golden wie die Sonne, eins so silbern wie der Mond und eins so glänzend wie die Sterne".

In einem norwegischen Märchen werden die Gestirne wie bei Goethe noch konkreter mit den Edelmetallen in Verbindung gebracht: In einem Schloss „östlich der Sonne und westlich des Mondes" befinden sich hier große Mengen von Gold und Silber. Das provenzalische Märchen *Woher Gold und Silber kommen* schildert eindrucksvoll die Entstehung der Edelmetalle: Der Teufel, so wird berichtet, schießt einen Pfeil auf die Sonne, „und der Herr Sonne schrie auf und Blut tropfte aus seiner Wunde und rann auf die Erde hinab und wurde dort zu Gold". Auch auf Frau Mond schießt der Teufel einen Pfeil, „und er traf sie in den Rücken, so dass Blut aus der Wunde spritzte, und das Blut tropfte auf die Erde und wurde zu Silber".

In dem Märchen *Sonnenblut und Mondblut* der in Argentinien lebenden Pirquita-Indianer wird die Entstehung von Gold und Silber folgendermaßen erklärt: Der Sonnenmann sticht sich „mit einer Smaragdnadel in den rechten Arm und das grüne Blut tropft in einen Becher aus Jaspis. Einige Tropfen fallen aber daran vorbei und hinunter auf die Erde, wo sie zu Gold werden." Das Menstruationsblut der Mondfrau wird in einer Schüssel aus Jade aufgefangen, wobei einige Tropfen verschüttet werden: „Die fallen auf die Erde und werden zu Silber. […] Und seitdem gibt es Gold von der Sonne – aber nur wenig, und Silber vom Mond – und das mehr."[15]

Vor solchen Hintergründen ist es naheliegend, dass es im Deutschen Stempelgesetz von 1884 zur Vorschrift wurde, Gegenstände aus Gold nicht nur mit der Reichskrone, sondern auch mit dem Sonnensymbol, und solche aus Silber auch mit der Mondsichel zu punzieren (Abb. 17).

Manche Märchen erzählen von den Gestirnen aber auch ohne Bezug zu den Edelmetallen. In Alexander Puschkins *Von der toten Prinzessin und den sieben Recken*, das eine gewisse Ähnlichkeit zu *Schneewittchen* aufweist, lässt der Autor den tapferen Jelissej die Sonne, dann den Mond und schließlich die Sterne befragen, wo seine von ihm verzweifelt gesuchte Geliebte zu finden sei. In dem märchenhaften Singspiel *Peterchens Mondfahrt* geht die Reise auf den Erdtrabanten. Und der Kleine Prinz von Antoine de Saint-Exupéry macht auf der Reise von seinem kleinen Asteroiden zur Erde auf einer ganzen Reihe von Planeten halt.

Zu den Meisterwerken der Weltliteratur gehören zwei Gedichte – beide in einem religiösen Kontext –, in denen die Sonne im Mittelpunkt steht: der *Sonnenhymnus* des Pharao Echnaton, der um 1360 vor Christus entstanden ist, und der *Sonnengesang* des heiligen Franziskus von Assisi aus dem Jahr 1225. Echnaton, der König beider Ägypten, rühmt zusammen mit seiner Gemahlin Nofretete die Sonne als den göttlichen Quell allen Lebens auf dieser Erde: „Schön erscheinst du im

16 *Sterntaler*, kolorierter Holzschnitt nach einer Zeichnung von Ludwig Richter, 1882. *Star Money*, coloured woodcut after a drawing by Ludwig Richter, 1882

In a Norwegian fairy tale, the heavenly bodies are linked even more specifically with precious metals as they are in Goethe: a great hoard of gold and silver is kept in a castle 'east of the Sun and west of the Moon'. The Provençal fairy tale *Where Gold and Silver Come From* tellingly describes the origin of the precious metals: the Devil, the story goes, shoots an arrow at the sun 'and Master Sun screamed and blood dripped from his wound and ran down to Earth and there it became gold'. And the Devil also shot an arrow at Mistress Moon, 'and he hit her in the back so that blood spurted from the wound, and the blood dripped to Earth and became silver'.

In the fairy tale *Sun Blood and Moon Blood* told by the Indians living in Pirquita, Argentina, the origin of silver and gold is explained as follows: The Sun Man pricks himself 'with an emerald needle in the right arm and the green blood drips into a jasper beaker. Some drops, however, drip past it and down to earth, where they become gold.' The Moon Woman's menstrual blood is caught in a jade bowl but some drops miss the bowl: 'They fall to Earth and become silver. [...] And since then there has been gold from the Sun – but only a little, and silver from the Moon – and more of it.'[15]

Against such a background, no wonder that the 1884 German Assay Law prescribed that objects made of gold had to be hallmarked not only with the imperial crown but also the sun symbol and silver objects with the crescent moon in addition to the imperial crown (Fig. 17).

Many fairy tales are about the heavenly bodies but are not associated with precious metals. In Aleksandr Pushkin's fairy-tale poem 'Tale of the Dead

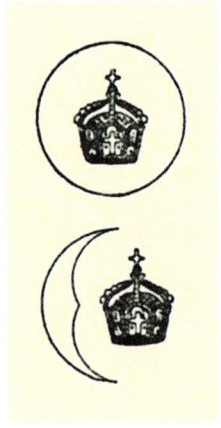

17 Gold- und Silberpunzen nach dem deutschen Stempelgesetz von 1884. Gold and silver hallmarks after the German Assay Law of 1884

Horizont des Himmels, du lebendige Sonne, die das Leben bestimmt […]. Deine Strahlen umfassen die Länder bis ans Ende von allem, was du geschaffen hast."[16]

Mehr als 2500 Jahre später dichtet Franziskus sein Gotteslob *Canticum Fratris Solis vel Laudes Creaturarum*, in dem er „dem höchsten, mächtigsten und guten Herrn" Ruhm, Ehre und Dank erweist: „Gelobt seist du, Herr, mit allen Wesen, die du geschaffen, der edlen Herrin vor allem, der Schwester Sonne, die uns den Tag herauf führt, und Licht mit ihren Strahlen, die Schöne, spendet; gar prächtig in mächtigem Glanze: dein Gleichnis ist sie, du Erhabener". Franziskus fährt fort: „Gelobt seist du, Herr, durch Bruder Mond und die Sterne; durch dich sie funkeln am Himmelsbogen und leuchten köstlich und schön."[17]

Fast ohne Zahl sind die Dichter, die – vornehmlich im 18. und 19., aber auch im 20. Jahrhundert – die Gestirne besungen haben: Man denke nur an Matthias Claudius (*Die Sternseherin Lise*), Friedrich Hölderlin (*Sonnenuntergang*), August Heinrich von Fallersleben (*Der Abendstern*), Heinrich Heine (*Auf den Wolken ruht der Mond*) oder Edmond Rostand (*Le Déjeuner du Soleil*).

Friedrich Schiller schreibt in seinem Gedicht *An die Sonne*: „Preis dir, die du dorten heraufstrahlst, Tochter des Himmels!/ Preis dem lieblichen Glanz/ Deines Lächelns, der alles begrüßet und alles erfreuet!" Und Ingeborg Bachmann würdigt die Sonne in einem gleichnamigen Gedicht mit den Worten: „Schöner als der beachtliche Mond und sein geadeltes Licht,/ Schöner als die Sterne, die berühmten Orden der Nacht,/ Viel schöner als der feurige Auftritt eines Kometen/ Und zu weit Schönrem berufen als jedes andre Gestirn,/ Weil dein und mein Leben jeden Tag an ihr hängt, ist die Sonne./ Schöne Sonne, die aufgeht, ihr Werk nicht vergessen hat […]".[18]

Schon in der Mitte des 17. Jahrhunderts hat Savinien Cyrano de Bergerac, der als einer der Begründer des Science-Fiction-Genres gilt, einen Roman und ein

Princess and the Seven Knights', which resembles *Snow White* in some respects, the author has courageous Yelisei ask the sun, then the moon and finally the stars where his beloved is, whom he is desperate to find. In *Peterchens Mondfahrt*, most recently translated as *Peter and Anneli's Journey to the Moon*, the journey goes to the earth's moon. And Antoine de Saint-Exupéry's *Le Petit Prince* [*The Little Prince*] stops at a number of planets on his journey to Earth on his little asteroid.

Two poems that are masterpieces of world literature – both in a religious context – in which the sun is invoked are the 'Hymn to the Sun' or 'Great Hymn to the Aten', composed by the pharaoh Akhenaten *c*.1360 BC, and the 'Canticum Fratris Solis vel Laudes Creaturarum' of St Francis of Assisi (1223–25). Akhenaten, King of the Two Egypts, joins his spouse, Nefertiti, in praising the sun as the divine source of all life on this earth: 'You rise in perfection on the horizon of the sky, / living Aten, who determines life. [...]. Your rays embrace the lands as far as everything you have made.'[16]

More than 2,500 years later, St Francis composed his 'Canticum Fratris Solis vel Laudes Creaturarum', usually called 'The Canticle of the Sun', in which he praises the 'Most high, all powerful, all good Lord! / All praise is Yours, all glory, all honour, and all blessing.' In a later stanza he adds: 'Be praised, my Lord, through all Your creatures, / especially through my lord Brother Sun, / who brings the day; and You give light through him. / And he is beautiful and radiant in all his splendour! / Of You, most High, he bears the likeness. / Be praised, my Lord, through Sister Moon and the stars; / In the heavens You have made them bright, precious and beautiful.'[17]

Countless poets have celebrated the heavenly bodies – chiefly in the eighteenth and nineteenth centuries but also in the twentieth century: German speakers would think of Matthias Claudius ('Die Sternseherin Lise' ['The Stargazer Lise']), Friedrich Hölderlin ('Sonnenuntergang' ['Sunset']), August Heinrich von Fallersleben ('Der Abendstern' ['The Evening Star']) and Heinrich Heine ('Auf den Wolken ruht der Mond' [The Moon Rests upon the Clouds']). French-speaking readers would remember Edmond Rostand ('Le Déjeuner du Soleil' [The Sun's Luncheon']).

In his poem to the sun, 'An die Sonne' ['To the Sun'], Friedrich Schiller writes, 'Praised beest thou, thou that art radiant there above, daughter of Heaven! / Praised be thy lovely Light / Praised be thy smile, which greeteth all and giveth joy to all!' And Ingeborg Bachmann honours the sun in a poem of that title as follows: 'Schöner als der beachtliche Mond und sein geadeltes Licht, / Schöner als die Sterne, die berühmten Orden der Nacht, / Viel schöner als der feurige Auftritt eines Kometen / Und zu weit Schönrem berufen als jedes andre Gestirn, / Weil dein und mein Leben jeden Tag an ihr hängt, ist die Sonne. / Schöne Sonne, die aufgeht, ihr Werk nicht vergessen hat [...].'[18]

By the mid-seventeenth century Savinien Cyrano de Bergerac, one of the modern founders (in the unbroken tradition of Lucian's *True History*) of science fiction as a genre, had written a novel and a fragmentary novel, in which he reported on voyages to the moon (*Les États et Empires de la Lune* [*The States and Empires of the Moon*]) and to the sun (*Les États et Empires du Soleil* [*The States and Empires of the Sun*]). His tales have been followed by the works of numerous followers in the fantasy genre, including Jules Verne (*De la Terre à la Lune* [*From the Earth to the Moon*], 1865, and *Autour de la Lune* [*Around the Moon*], 1870). Jacques Offenbach made use of the material from the Jules Verne novels in the operetta

Romanfragment verfasst, in denen er von der Reise zum Mond (*Les États et Empires de la Lune*) und der Reise zur Sonne (*Les États et Empires du Soleil*) berichtet. Seine Erzählungen fanden viele Nachfolger in der phantastischen Literatur, etwa in den Romanen von Jules Verne (*De la Terre à la Lune*, 1865, oder *Autour de la Lune*, 1870). Jacques Offenbach hat Jules Vernes Stoff in seiner 1875 komponierten Operette *Le Voyage de la Lune* frei verwendet. 1902 war er die Vorlage für den gleichnamigen Film von Georges Méliès. Von Verne stammt außerdem der Roman *Hector Servadac. Voyages et Aventures à travers le Monde solaire* (1878).

Die Aufzählung phantastischer Literatur zu Sonne, Mond und Sternen ließe sich beliebig fortsetzen – etwa bis zu Durs Grünbeins Gedichtzyklus *Cyrano oder die Rückkehr vom Mond*, in dem fast jedes der Gedichte vom Mond, gelegentlich auch von der Sonne und den Sternen handelt. Oder bis hin zu den Mangas der japanischen Zeichnerin Naoko Takeuchi. In *Sailor Moon* beispielsweise bemüht sich das tollpatschige Mädchen Usaki Tsakino, genannt Bunny, mit der Unterstützung der Mondprinzessin und weiterer galaktischer Helfer, das Böse im Universum zu besiegen.

Fritz Lang hat bereits 1928/29 den phantastischen Film *Die Frau im Mond* gedreht, dessen Handlung darauf beruht, dass die auf der Rückseite des Mondes vermuteten Goldvorkommen erforscht werden sollen, und auch der Lügenbaron Münchhausen hatte – in einem Film von 1943 mit Hans Albers in der Titelrolle – einige Abenteuer auf dem Mond zu bestehen.

Auch Zeitschriften und Tageszeitungen tragen die Sonne und die Sterne im Namen: In Deutschland ist das Magazin *stern* besonders populär (Abb. 18). In England sind es beispielsweise die Boulevardzeitung *The Sun* und der *Morning Star*. Den Abendstern tragen viele englischsprachige Zeitungen im Namen wie beispielsweise der bis 1981 in Amerika erschienene *Washington Evening Star*. Vom sowjetischen Verteidigungsministerium wurde seit 1924 die Militärzeitung *Roter Stern* herausgegeben.

Kunsthandwerk
Wenn die Gestirne in vielen Mythen und Religionen, in der bildenden Kunst, in der Musik und Literatur ihren mannigfachen Niederschlag gefunden haben, ist es nicht verwunderlich, dass sie auch im sogenannten Kunsthandwerk in Erscheinung treten. Auf die berühmten Tapisserien und Keramiken von Jean Lurçat wurde bereits hingewiesen. Tausende von Jahren zuvor – in der Bronzezeit – entstanden die Goldenen Hüte von Schifferstadt (13./12. Jahrhundert v. Chr.) und von Ezelsdorf (11.–9. Jahrhundert v. Chr.); ebenso die Goldschale von Zürich-Altstetten (zwischen 1500 und 1000 v. Chr.; Abb. 19) und die goldene Schale aus dem Schatz von Eberswalde (10.–9. Jahrhundert v. Chr.), auf denen die Wissenschaft die Zeichen der Sonne und des Mondes erkennt.

18   Titelblatt des Magazins *stern*, Nr. 41, 6.10.1983. Front page of *stern* magazine, No. 41, 6.10.1983

Le Voyage de la Lune [*A Trip to the Moon*], which he composed in 1875. The content was the model for the 1902 Georges Méliès film of the same title. Another Jules Verne science fiction novel on the subject of a voyage in space is *Hector Servadac. Voyages et Aventures à travers le Monde solaire* (1877–78), translated into English as *Off on a Comet*.

The roll of fantasy literature in several genres about the sun, moon and stars is endless – including Durs Grünbein's cycle of poems *Cyrano oder die Rückkehr vom Mond* [*Cyrano or Return to the Moon*], in which almost all are about the moon and some about the sun and the stars. Or the manga series by the Japanese artist Naoko Takeuchi. In *Sailor Moon*, for instance, an awkward girl named Usaki Tsakino, Bunny for short, tries to conquer evil in the universe, supported by the Moon Princess and other galactic helpers.

As early as 1928/29 Fritz Lang made a silent science fiction film, *Die Frau im Mond* [*Woman in the Moon*]. The plot is based on exploring the far side of the moon to look for gold. Baron Münchausen, prince of liars, also had some adventures on the moon – in *Münchhausen*, an iconic 1943 Ufa colour film with Hans Albers in the title role.

Magazines and newspapers also display the sun and stars in their titles: a particularly popular one in Germany is *stern* magazine (Fig. 18). In the UK newspapers such as the *Sun*, on the far right, and the *Morning Star*, on the far left, have between them polarised the tabloid spectrum. Many English-language newspapers invoke the Evening Star in their titles, including the *Washington Evening Star*, an afternoon daily published in America until 1981. Since 1924 the *Red Star* has been the official paper of the Soviet Ministry of Defence and its Russian successor.

19 Goldschale mit Darstellungen von Sonne und Mond, gefunden in Zürich-Altstetten, Schweiz, zwischen 1500 und 1000 v. Chr., Gold, H 12 cm, Dm 25 cm. Gold bowl with sun and moon, found in Zurich-Altstetten, Switzerland, between 1500 and 1000 BC, gold, H 12 cm, dia. 25 cm. Schweizerisches Nationalmuseum, Zürich, Inv. A-86063

Der sogenannte *Sonnenwagen von Trundholm* aus der älteren nordischen Bronzezeit (um 1400 v. Chr.) hatte mit Sicherheit einen kultischen Hintergrund.[19] Die goldene Larnax aus dem 4. Jahrhundert v. Chr., die möglicherweise die Gebeine Philipps II., des Vaters Alexanders des Großen, enthielt und sich heute im Museum von Vergina befindet, zeigt ein Gestirn, das als *Sonne von Vergina* die Flagge des modernen Staates Mazedonien ziert.

Nur als literarisches Bild erhalten hat sich der Schild des Achilles. Homer beschreibt im 18. Gesang der *Ilias* das vom göttlichen Schmied Hephaistos gearbeitete Werk: „Drauf nun schuf er die Erd' und das wogende Meer und den Himmel, auch den vollen Mond und die rastlos laufende Sonne; drauf auch alle Gestirne, die den Himmel umleuchten."

Um 1480 schuf der Bildschnitzer Erasmus Grasser eine Sonne für das alte Rathaus in München, während nur wenige Jahre später der Holzbildhauer Veit Stoß

Artefacts and applied arts

Since the heavenly bodies appear in so many guises in myths and religions, in fine art, music and literature, it is hardly surprising that they also figure prominently in what is known as the applied arts. The famous Aubusson tapestries and ceramic work of Jean Lurçat's have already been touched on. The gold hats of Schifferstadt (thirteenth/twelfth centuries BC) and Ezelsdorf (eleventh–ninth centuries BC), the gold bowl of Zurich-Altstetten (1500–1000 BC; Fig. 19) and the gold bowl from the Eberswalde Hoard (tenth/ninth centuries BC) were made thousands of years before Lurçat – in the Bronze Age. Archaeologists have recognised signs for the sun and moon on all of them.

The find known as the 'Trundholm sun chariot' from the early Nordic Bronze Age (c.1400 BC) definitely had a cultic background.[19] The gold larnax from the fourth century BC, which may have contained the bones of Philip II of Macedon, father of Alexander the Great, and is now in the museum at Vergina, is decorated with a celestial configuration that is also emblazoned on the flag of the modern country of Macedonia as the Sun of Vergina.

The Shield of Achilles, on the other hand, has only survived as literary imagery. In Book 18 of the *Iliad*, Homer describes it as the work of Hephaistos, blacksmith to the gods: 'On it he made the Earth and the sea surge and the sky, also the full moon and the tireless Sun; also all the heavenly bodies that wreathe the sky.'

About 1480 the woodcarver Erasmus Grasser made a sun for Munich Town Hall. Only a few years later Veit Stoß, a sculptor in wood, added a golden sun to the reverse of a rosary medallion on the *Angelic Salutation* in the Church of St Lorenz in Nuremberg. The silver-gilt crown (latter half of the fifteenth century) of the Madonna from the Catedral de Castelló d'Empúries – it is now kept in the Museu d'Art in Girona – shows, on the other hand, a circle of stars. It alludes to the crown of stars upon the head of the Woman of the Apocalypse in Chapter 12 of the Book of Revelation.[20]

The Sun King, Louis XIV of France, who in his youth performed in ballet as the personification of the sun (Fig. 20),[21] had his face framed by the sun's rays to attest to the legitimacy of his claim to rule by 'the divine right of kings'. In 1709 the Dresden goldsmith Johann Melchior Dinglinger made a sun mask – bearing the likeness of Augustus the Strong, Elector of Saxony and King of Poland (Fig. 23). Dinglinger was also the creator of a multi-figure masterpiece of Baroque goldsmithing known as *Der Thron des Großmoguls Aureng-Zeb* [*The Throne of the Grand Mogul Aurangzeb*]: the monarch is seated beneath the gold rays of the sun in this large group of figures.[22]

Precious sun monstrances were made from the early Baroque era on into the twentieth century, as exemplified by one such piece made in Vienna by Heinrich Anders in 1894 (Fig. 22). The moon usually functions as a 'lunula' as the container for the host on monstrances of this kind.

In 1900 the Paris jeweller Joseph Chaumet made a liturgical object reminiscent of a monstrance without really being one; he called it *Christus Vincit* and it is surmounted by the configuration known as a 'sunburst' of diamond rays radiating from a triangular sapphire. Salvador Dalí produced a design for a cross set with precious stones, with a sunburst at the centre: it bears the name *The Light of Christ*.[23]

auf der Rückseite eines Rosenkranzmedaillons des *Englischen Grußes* in der Lorenzkirche zu Nürnberg eine goldene Sonne anbrachte. Die aus der zweiten Hälfte des 15. Jahrhunderts stammende silbervergoldete Krone der Madonna aus der Catedral de Castelló d'Empúries – sie wird heute im Museu d'Art in Girona aufbewahrt – zeigt hingegen einen Sternenkranz. Er nimmt Bezug auf die Sternenkrone des apokalyptischen Weibes aus der Offenbarung des Johannes.[20]

Der Sonnenkönig Ludwig XIV., der schon als Kind in einem Ballett als Personifikation der Sonne aufgetreten war (Abb. 20),[21] ließ sein Antlitz von Sonnenstrahlen umrahmen, um auf diese Weise den Anspruch auf seine „Gottgleichheit" zu dokumentieren. Im Jahre 1709 schuf auch der Dresdener Goldschmied Johann Melchior Dinglinger eine Sonnenmaske – allerdings mit dem Bildnis des sächsischen Kurfürsten und Königs von Polen August des Starken (Abb. 23). Von Dinglinger stammt außerdem eines der Hauptwerke barocker Goldschmiedekunst, der sogenannte *Thron des Großmoguls Aureng-Zeb*; der Herrscher sitzt dort unter einer goldstrahlenden Sonne.[22]

Seit der frühen Barockzeit und bis ins 20. Jahrhundert wurden kostbare Sonnenmonstranzen hergestellt, wie beispielsweise ein Exemplar, das im Jahre 1894 von Heinrich Anders in Wien geschaffen worden ist (Abb. 22). Der Mond spielt bei solchen Monstranzen üblicherweise als „Lunula" die Rolle des Hostienträgers.

Der Pariser Juwelier Joseph Chaumet schuf im Jahre 1900 einen sakralen Gegenstand, der an eine Monstranz erinnert, ohne wirklich eine solche zu sein; *Christus Vincit* nannte er dieses Objekt, das bekrönt ist von einem sogenannten „Sunburst" aus Diamantstrahlen, die von einem dreieckigen Safir ausgehen. Von Salvador Dalí stammt außerdem der Entwurf für ein mit Edelsteinen geschmücktes Kreuz, in dessen Zentrum ein Sunburst steht; es trägt den Namen *The Light of Christ*.[23]

In den Werkstätten des Petersburger Juweliers Carl Fabergé entstand – neben einem silbernen Feuerzeug in Form einer liegenden Mondsichel – auch eine Dose aus Nephrit, die ebenfalls das Sunburst-Motiv zeigt (Abb. 82). Die Kunstfertigkeit Fabergés und seiner Werkmeister stellen aber auch Tisch- und Wanduhren mit Mond- und Sternenmotiven unter Beweis (s. Abb. 87); sie sind teilweise aus vergoldetem Silber, mit Email verziert und mit Diamanten besetzt.

Reizvoll ist auch der von René Lalique entworfene Flakon für das Parfum *Dans la nuit*, der sowohl mit einem Sternenhimmel als auch mit einer Mondsichel geschmückt ist (Abb. 21). Der im Wesentlichen für Tiffany in New York tätige französische Schmuckdesigner Jean Schlumberger schuf in den 1950er-Jahren das Zeremonialschwert für ein Mitglied der Académie Française, den Dramatiker Marcel Achard. Am Griff des Schwertes befindet sich eine goldene Mondsichel.[24]

Einen religiösen Hintergrund hat der sogenannte *Herrnhuter Stern*, eine Entwicklung der Herrnhuter Brüdergemeine aus den frühen 19. Jahrhundert.

20 Der junge Ludwig XIV., König von Frankreich, in der Rolle des Apoll im *Ballet royal de la nuit* von Jean Baptiste Lully, nach 1653, kolorierte Zeichnung. The young Louis XIV, King of France, in the role of Apollo in the *Ballet royal de la nuit* by Jean Baptiste Lully, after 1653, hand-coloured drawing. Bibliothèque nationale de France, Paris

A nephrite box, also bearing the sunburst motif, was made in the workshops of the Saint Petersburg jeweller Carl Fabergé (see Fig. 82) — along with a silver cigarette lighter in the form of a recumbent crescent moon. The consummate skill possessed by Fabergé and his workmasters is also attested by table and wall clocks featuring moon and star motifs (see Fig. 87), some of which are silver-gilt decorated with enamel and set with diamonds.

The stopper of the appealing flacon designed by René Lalique for the perfume *Dans la nuit* is decorated with both a starry sky and a crescent moon (Fig. 21). In the 1950s the French designer Jean Schlumberger, who worked mainly for Tiffany in New York, designed a ceremonial sword for the dramatist Marcel Achard, a member of the Académie française. The pommel of the sword is decorated with a gold crescent moon.[24]

The ornament known as the *Herrnhuter Stern* (Moravian star) has a religious background. It was developed by the Herrnhut Brotherhood in the early nineteenth century. Originally consisting of 110 rays, it is still used in many churches and private households as a decoration at Advent and Christmas — usually in a much simplified form. Variants of this motif have featured as Swarovski crystal Christmas-tree decorations. Since 2004 Michael Hammers from Aachen has used this glittering material to surmount what is probably the most famous Christmas tree in the world in front of the Rockefeller Center in New York with a star that is three metres high. Innsbruck, too, now has a Swarovski star by Hammers.

21 René Lalique, Parfumflakon *Dans la nuit*, Flakon und Stöpsel mit Sternen und Mondsichel, in Verwendung bis 1924, Glas, H 7,5 cm (Flakon). René Lalique, perfume bottle *Dans la nuit*, presentation, flacon and stopper with stars and crescent moon, in use until 1924, glass, H 7.5 cm (flacon). Courtesy of Foundation Silvio Denz

22 Heinrich Anders, Sonnenmonstranz, Wien, um 1894, Silber, vergoldet, H 40 cm. Heinrich Anders, monstrance, Vienna, *c.*1894, silver-gilt, H 40 cm.
KHM-Museumsverband, Wien, Inv. SK GS B 12

Ursprünglich aus 110 Strahlen bestehend, wird er zur Advents- und Weihnachtszeit noch heute in vielen Kirchen und privaten Haushalten präsentiert – meist in vereinfachter Form. Abgewandelt erscheint dieses Motiv als kristallener Swarovski-Christbaumschmuck. Seit 2004 verwendet Michael Hammers aus Aachen dieses glitzernde Material, um den wohl berühmtesten Weihnachtsbaum der Welt vor dem Rockefeller Center in New York mit einem drei Meter großen Stern zu bekrönen. Auch Innsbruck verfügt inzwischen über einen Swarovski-Hammers-Stern.

Breit ist das Spektrum der Ausdrucksformen, in denen die Menschen sich mit den Gestirnen auseinandersetzen. Die nur unvollständige und skizzenhafte Darstellung anhand von Beispielen aus Religion, Mythen und Märchen, aus Heraldik, Literatur, Musik, bildender Kunst und Kunsthandwerk und manch anderem Gebiet mag hier einen ersten Einblick geben. Auf das weite Feld der Naturwissenschaften – Astronomie, Chemie, Physik, Weltraumfahrt und Weltraumtechnik beispielsweise – kann in diesem Zusammenhang lediglich hingewiesen, nicht aber eingegangen werden.

Vielgestaltig treten die Sonne, der Mond und die Sterne auch im Bereich des Schmucks auf: von früher Vorzeit bis in die Gegenwart, magisch beeinflusst oder in dekorativer Gestalt, in vielen Kulturen und Regionen, fast überall auf dieser Welt. Diesem wahrhaft faszinierenden Phänomen sollen die folgenden Kapitel gewidmet sein.

The range of forms of expression in which the heavenly bodies figure prominently is indeed broad. Of necessity incomplete, indeed sketchy, this brief survey drawing on examples taken from religion, myth and fairy tale, heraldry, literature, music, fine art, the applied arts and more is intended to give only an introductory glimpse. In the present connection, the wide field of the physical sciences – astronomy, chemistry, physics, space exploration and space technology – can only be mentioned in passing without being handled in depth.

The sun, moon and stars also appear in many forms in the field of jewellery: from early prehistoric times to the present, under the sway of magic or in decorative guise, in many cultures and religions, virtually everywhere in the world. The following chapters are devoted to this truly fascinating phenomenon.

23 Johann Melchior Dinglinger, Sonnenmaske mit Gesichtszügen Augusts II. des Starken, Dresden, 1709, Kupfer, getrieben, vergoldet, Messing, vergoldet, H 49 cm, B 46,1 cm. Johann Melchior Dinglinger, sun mask with the facial features of August II (the Strong), Dresden, 1709, chased copper-gilt, brass-gilt, H 49 cm, W 46.1 cm. Staatliche Kunstsammlungen Dresden, Inv. N 171

ÄGYPTEN

Sie ließen sich als Söhne der Götter verehren und schmückten sich mit entsprechenden Zeichen und Symbolen – die Mächtigen, die Herrscher im alten Ägypten. Im Lande der Pharaonen war es vornehmlich die Sonne, die sich im Schmuck der Könige und ihrer Familien sowie in den Kleinodien der Priesterschaft und der hohen Beamten manifestierte. Unter Echnaton (Neues Reich, 18. Dynastie), auf dessen Sonnenhymnus bereits hingewiesen wurde (s. S. 32), stand Aton – einst Gott der Abendsonne, nun oberstes göttliches Wesen – im Mittelpunkt der Verehrung. Auf Reliefs und Darstellungen aus edlen Metallen und Edelsteinen spendet er, dargestellt als Sonnenscheibe, dem Pharao mit Gemahlin und Familie seine Gnade und seinen Segen.

Als Attribut des Re-Harachte, des Gottes der Morgensonne, findet sich die Sonnenscheibe etwa auf zahlreichen Preziosen, die nur wenige Jahre nach Echnatons Tod dem jugendlichen König Tutanchamun (Neues Reich, 18. Dynastie) ins Grab gegeben wurden. Auf einem Fingerring aus massivem Gold beispielsweise erscheint der als wesensgleich mit Horus angesehene Gott in Gestalt eines falkenköpfigen Mannes mit der Sonnenscheibe über dem Haupt. Auch als Falke selbst tritt Re-Harachte – immer von der Sonne bekrönt – auf Reliefs, Wandmalereien und auf zahlreichen Schmuckstücken in Erscheinung (Abb. 24).

Die Hieroglyphe des offiziellen Königsnamens Tutanchamuns, die gelegentlich auf Fayenceringen zu sehen ist, zeigt die Sonne zusammen mit dem heiligen Käfer Skarabäus, was die kultische Nähe des jung verstorbenen Königs zu den göttlichen Mächten beweist (Abb. 26). Auch ein goldener Siegelring des Pharao Ramses II. aus der 19. Dynastie, der um 1250 v. Chr. datiert wird, trägt das Sonnensymbol als Bestandteil des königlichen Namens (Abb. 25).

Der Skarabäus, in der Mythologie gleichgesetzt mit Chepre, der als Gottheit ebenfalls die aufgehende Sonne symbolisiert, spielte in der Welt des Glaubens eine ganz besondere Rolle. Als Symbol der Wiedergeburt und des ewigen Lebens ziert er mehrere Pektoralien und Armschmuckstücke, die zu den Grabbeigaben des Tutanchamun gehören.[25] Auf diesen Schmuckstücken ist die göttliche Sonne häufig – jedoch nicht ausschließlich – als Karneol in runder goldener Fassung dargestellt. So beispielsweise im Falle eines großen geflügelten Skarabäus, der die Sonnenscheibe in den vorderen Gliedmaßen hält.

Nach ihrem Untergang im Westen wird die Sonne, auf Schmuckstücken gelegentlich begleitet von einem Skarabäus, durch die Unterwelt geleitet, um am nächsten Morgen im Osten wieder aufzugehen. Diese mythische Reise ist eindrucksvoll dargestellt auf einem Pektorale der 22. Dynastie aus dem 9. vorchristlichen Jahrhundert. Die von einer Barke getragene Sonne wird darauf von einem gravierten Lapislazuli repräsentiert, auf dem die Darstellung des Pharaos Amun-Re zu sehen ist.[26] Ein über dieser Szene befindlicher balkenartiger Streifen

24 Ring mit der Darstellung des Sonnengottes Re-Harachte, Grabbeigabe des Tutanchamun, Theben, Ägypten, Neues Reich, 18. Dynastie, 14. Jh. v. Chr., Gold. Ring featuring the sun god Ra-Harakhte, burial object of Tutankhamun, Thebes, Egypt, New Kingdom, 18th dynasty, 14th century BC, gold. Egyptian Museum, Cairo

EGYPT

They had themselves venerated as the sons of gods and adorned themselves with the signs and symbols to match that status – the mighty who reigned in ancient Egypt. In the land of the pharaohs, it was chiefly the sun that was featured in the jewellery worn by kings and their families as well as the treasures owned by the priest caste and high-ranking officials. In the reign of Akhenaten (18th dynasty, New Kingdom), whose *Hymn to the Sun* has been mentioned (see p. 35), Aton – once the god of the evening sun, now the highest divine being – was the focus of veneration. In reliefs and representations in noble metals and gemstones, he is represented as the disc of the sun, bestowing his mercy and his blessings on the pharaoh with his spouse and family.

As the attribute of Ra-Harakhte, god of the morning sun, the sun disc occurs on, for instance, the numerous precious grave goods placed in the tomb of the young king Tutankhamun (18th dynasty, New Kingdom) only a few years after Akhenaten's death. On a solid gold finger ring, for instance, the god, who was viewed as coessentially Horus, appears as a falcon-headed human figure with the sun disc above his head. Ra-Harakhte – always crowned with the sun – also appears as a falcon in reliefs, frescoes and numerous pieces of jewellery (Fig. 24).

The official titular hieroglyph of Tutankhamun's throne name, which is occasionally encountered on faience rings, shows the sun together with *Scarabaeus sacer*, the sacred scarab beetle, a juxtaposition that proves the cultic affinities of the king who died young with the divine powers (Fig. 26). A gold seal

25 Siegelring Ramses II., wohl aus dem Grab Ramses II., Ägypten, Neues Reich, 19. Dynastie, um 1250 v. Chr., Gold, Siegelplatte 2,95 cm. Signet ring of Rameses II, probably from the tomb of Rameses II, Egypt, New Kingdom, 19th dynasty, c.1250 BC, gold, signet 2.95 cm. Staatliches Museum Ägyptischer Kunst, München, Inv. ÄS 5851

26 Siegelring mit Hieroglyphe des Königsnamens Tutanchamuns, Grabbeigabe, Ägypten, Neues Reich, 18. Dynastie, Mitte 14. Jh. v. Chr., glasierter Ton.
Signet ring with hieroglyph of King Tutankhamun's name, burial object, Egypt, New Kingdom, 18th dynasty, mid-14th century BC, glazed terracotta.
Schmuckmuseum Pforzheim, Inv. 1963/8

ring owned by the pharaoh Ramses II (19th dynasty), which is dated c.1250 BC, also bears the sun symbol as a constituent of the king's throne name (Fig. 25).

The scarab beetle, which in ancient Egyptian mythology is identical to Khepri, who also symbolises the rising sun as a deity, played a very special role in ancient Egyptian religion. As the symbol of rebirth and eternal life, the scarab beetle adorns several pectorals and pieces of arm jewellery that were found among the grave goods in Tutankhamun's tomb.[25] On these pieces of jewellery, the divine sun is often – but not always – represented as a carnelian in a round gold setting – for instance, in the case of a large, winged scarab beetle holding the sun disc in its front legs.

After setting in the west, the sun, on pieces of jewellery occasionally accompanied by a scarab beetle, was conveyed through the realm of the dead to rise again in the east the following morning. This mythical journey is impressively depicted on a pectoral (22nd dynasty) from the ninth century BC. Conveyed by a boat, the sun is represented on the pectoral engraved on a piece of lapis lazuli, on which the pharaoh Amun-Ra is portrayed.[26] Studded with numerous minute stars, a beam-like strip above this scene symbolises the night, during which the sun journeys through the realm of the dead.

Two pieces of neck jewellery from Dahshur that were once owned by Princess Khnumet also verify that stars appear, at least occasionally, in jewellery associated with ancient Egypt. These treasures (12th dynasty) date from the

symbolisiert mit zahlreichen kleinen Sternen die Nacht, während der die Sonnenreise durch die Unterwelt stattfindet.

Dass Sterne im Schmuck des altägyptischen Umfeldes zumindest gelegentlich in Erscheinung traten, lässt sich auch anhand zweier Halsschmuckstücke der Prinzessin Chnumet aus Dahshur nachweisen. Es handelt sich hierbei um Preziosen aus der 12. Dynastie des frühen 2. Jahrtausends v. Chr. Ihre Stilistik und Handwerkstechnik ist allerdings nicht rein ägyptisch, sondern dürfte auf Einflüsse aus der ägäischen Kultur oder aus Mesopotamien zurückzuführen sein.[27]

Der üblicherweise als Falke dargestellte Gott Horus (s. auch S. 46), ein Sohn des Osiris und der Isis, war ein wichtiger Bestandteil sowohl des altägyptischen Sonnen- als auch des Mondkultes. So wurden die Augen des Horus mit Sonne und Mond identifiziert. Auf einem Pektorale aus dem Grab des Tutanchamun wie auch auf einem goldenen Ring des gleichen Schatzes trägt Horus – mit Re-Harachte gleichgesetzt – die Sonnenscheibe über dem Haupt (Abb. 27).

Göttliche Huld und göttliche Gnade spiegeln sich in der Kunst und im kostbaren Schmuck des alten Ägypten: Die Sonne als Spender aller Wohltaten ist dafür das sichtbare Zeichen.

ALTER ORIENT

Auch im Zweistromland zwischen Euphrat und Tigris, im alten Assyrien, verehrten die mächtigen Herrscher die Sonne, den Mond und die Sterne als Gnade und Segen bringende Gottheiten. Man sah sie als Bürgen für persönliches Glück sowie politischen Erfolg und betete sie an – zum eigenen Wohl und zum Wohle der Untertanen. Bei archäologischen Ausgrabungen entdeckte Inschriften und Reliefbildwerke legen davon ein markantes Zeugnis ab. Sie stellen den assyrischen König Assur-nasirpal II. dar, der in der ersten Hälfte des 9. vorchristlichen Jahrhunderts in der Hauptstadt Nimrud residierte. Eines der Reliefs zeigt den Herrscher, wie er auf mehrere kultische Symbole deutet, darunter die Sonne, den Mond und einen Stern; auf der Brust trägt der König die Zeichen seiner Macht.[28] In einem anderen Relief sind die Zeichen, die den Rang und die Verbundenheit mit den Gestirnen symbolisieren, zu Anhängern seines Halsschmuckes geworden (s. Abb. 2).

Schon lange vor Assur-nasirpal II., bereits zu Beginn des 2. Jahrtausends v. Chr., sind Sonne und Mond als magische Motive belegt, beispielsweise auf mesopotamischen Rollsiegeln. Auch der sogenannte Dilbat-Halsschmuck zeigt zusammen mit anderen goldenen Anhängern drei granulierte Sonnenscheiben und eine Mondsichel.[29] Ein Relief aus Susa – es wird in das 12. Jahrhundert v. Chr. datiert – bezeugt auf eindrucksvolle Weise die Verehrung der Himmelskörper: Über drei

27 Falken-Pektorale aus dem Grab Tutanchamuns, Ägypten, Neues Reich, 18. Dynastie, 14. Jh. v. Chr., Gold mit Einlagen aus Lapislazuli, Türkis, Karneol und Glas, B 12,6 cm. Falcon pectoral from the tomb of Tutankhamun, Egypt, New Kingdom, 18th dynasty, 14th century BC, gold inlaid with lapis lazuli, turquoise, carnelian and glass, W 12.6 cm. Egyptian National Museum, Cairo

28 Kudurru (Grenzstein) des Melischichu in Erinnerung an eine Landstiftung für seine Tochter Hunnubat-Nannaya, Hillah, Mesopotamien, kassitische Dynastie, 12 Jh. v. Chr., Kalkstein, 83 × 42 cm. Kudurru (boundary stone) of Melišishu in remembrance of a land trust for his daughter Hunnubat-Nannaya, Hillah, Mesopotamia, Kassite dynasty, 12th century BC, limestone, 83 × 42 cm. Musée du Louvre, Paris, Département des Antiquités orientales, Inv. SB23

early second millennium BC. Stylistically they are not purely Egyptian, nor is the technique employed to make them. Instead these stylistic and technical differences are probably due to influences from Aegean culture or Mesopotamia.[27]

Usually depicted as a falcon, the god Horus (also see p. 47), a son of Osiris and Isis, was an important element of the ancient Egyptian cults of both the sun and the moon. Thus Horus's eyes were equated with the sun and moon. On a pectoral from Tutankhamun's tomb and a gold ring from the same treasure, Horus – identical with Ra-Harakhte – is wearing the sun disc above his head (Fig. 27).

Divine benevolence and mercy are reflected in the art and the precious jewellery of ancient Egypt: the sun as the bestower of all beneficence is the visible sign of this.

THE ANCIENT NEAR EAST

The powerful rulers of Mesopotamia between the rivers Euphrates and Tigris also venerated the sun, the moon and the stars as deities who bestowed mercy and blessings. Since they saw the heavenly bodies as guarantors of personal good fortune as well as political success, they worshipped them – for their own good and that of their subjects. Inscriptions and reliefs discovered in archaeological excavations testify memorably that this was so. They represent the Assyrian king Assur-nasirpal II, who ruled from Nimrud, his capital, in the first half of the ninth century BC. One of the reliefs shows the ruler pointing to several cult symbols, including the sun, the moon and a star; on his breast the king is wearing the emblems of his power.[28] In another relief the signs symbolising the ruler's status and his affinities with the heavenly bodies have become pendants on his neck jewellery (see Fig. 2).

Long before Assur-nasirpal II, in the early second millennium BC, there is evidence of the sun and moon as magical motifs – for instance, on Mesopotamian cylinder seals. The find known as the Dilbat necklace features three granulated sun discs and a crescent moon alongside other gold pendants.[29] A relief from Susa – it is dated to the twelfth century BC – impressively attests to the veneration of heavenly bodies: above three figures represented in profile – on the left the goddess Nana is enthroned, with the Kassite king Melišishu and his daughter standing in front of her – an eight-pointed star, a recumbent crescent moon and a sun disc can be seen, all of them on a larger scale (Fig. 28). A round pendant of sheet gold, also bearing an eight-pointed star, was found at excavations in Tell al-Rimah; the pendant is dated to the mid-thirteenth century BC.[30] Scholars have not yet clarified beyond all doubt whether the motifs on such pieces of jewellery are suns or stars; nonetheless, the magical-mythical connection is undisputed. By contrast, a piece of neck jewellery excavated at Berikldeebe near Shida Kartli in the Caucasus consists of nine gold crescent moons. It is dated to the fourteenth to thirteenth centuries BC.[31] Moreover, the jewellery finds of Ras Shamra, dated to the fourteenth to thirteenth centuries, indicate

29 Anhänger mit Astralmotiv (der Planet Venus), Ras Shamra-Ugarit, Syrien, 14.–13. Jh. v. Chr., Gold. Pendant with astral motif (the planet Venus), Ras Shamra-Ugarit, Syria, 14th–13th century BC, gold. Musée du Louvre, Paris, Département des Antiquités orientales, Inv. AO 17363

30 Lunula-Anhänger, Ras Shamra-Ugarit, Syrien, 14.–13. Jh. v. Chr., Gold. Lunula pendant, Ras Shamra-Ugarit, Syria, 14th–13th century BC, gold. Musée du Louvre, Paris, Département des Antiquités orientales, Inv. AO 19134

im Profil dargestellten Figuren – links thront die Göttin Nana, vor ihr stehen der kassitische König Melischichu und seine Tochter – sind großformatig ein achtstrahliger Stern, eine liegende Mondsichel und eine Sonnenscheibe zu sehen (Abb. 28). Ein runder Anhänger aus Goldblech, ebenfalls mit achtstrahligem Stern, wurde bei Ausgrabungen in Tell-al-Rimah gefunden; er wird in die Mitte des 13. Jahrhunderts v. Chr. datiert.[30] Ob es sich bei solchen Schmuckstücken um Sonnen- oder Sternmotive handelt, hat die Wissenschaft noch nicht eindeutig geklärt, der magisch-mythische Zusammenhang ist jedoch unbestritten. Ein in Berikldeebe bei Schida Kartli im Kaukasus ausgegrabener Halsschmuck besteht hingegen aus neun goldenen Mondsicheln; er wird in das 14. bis 13. Jahrhundert v. Chr. datiert.[31] Auch die Schmuckfunde von Ras Shamra, die in das 14. und 13. Jahrhundert datiert werden, lassen erkennen, dass in dem dort blühenden kanaanitischen Stadtstaat Ugarit im heutigen Syrien die Sonne und der Mond kultische Verehrung erfahren haben (Abb. 29, 30).

31 Statuette einer nackten, stehenden Frau, vielleicht die babylonische Göttin Ishtar, Babylon, 3. Jh. v. Chr.–3. Jh. n. Chr., Alabaster, Gold, Rubine, Ton, H 24,8 cm. Statuette of a naked woman standing, possibly the Babylonian goddess Ishtar, Babylon, 3rd century BC–3 century AD, alabaster, gold, rubies, terracotta, H 24.8 cm. Musée du Louvre, Paris, Département des Antiquités orientales, Inv. AO 20127

Die große Popularität der Sonnen- beziehungsweise Sternanhänger kann vielleicht auf die altorientalischen Göttinnen Astarte und Ishtar zurückgeführt werden, die beide sowohl mit der Sonne und den Sternen als auch mit dem Mond in Verbindung gebracht wurden. Eine antike Statuette zeigt möglicherweise die mit Venus zu identifizierende mesopotamische Ishtar mit einer nach oben offenen Mondsichel auf dem Haupt (Abb. 31).

Im nordwestlichen Persien existierte im Zagros-Gebirge die sogenannte Luristan-Kultur, die vornehmlich durch ihre faszinierenden Bronzeobjekte ausgezeichnet ist. Unter dem Einfluss anderer frühorientalischer Zivilisationen schufen die Bronzegießer dieser Region auch Schmuckstücke, die – aller Wahrscheinlichkeit nach als Kultgegenstände – die Gestirne zum magischen Inhalt hatten.

32   Ring mit Darstellung des Sternenhimmels, Luristan, Persien, frühes 1. Jahrtausend v. Chr., Bronze.   Ring featuring the star-lit sky, Luristan, Persia, early first millennium BC, bronze.
Schmuckmuseum Pforzheim, Inv. 1969/43

33 Siegelring mit einem vermutlich die Plejaden anbetenden Priester, achämenidisch, Persien, 6. Jh. v. Chr., Bronze. Signet ring with priest worshipping what appear to be the Pleiades, Achaemenid, Persia, 6th century BC, bronze. Schmuckmuseum Pforzheim, Inv. 1969/44

that in the then flourishing Canaanite city state of Ugarit, in present-day Syria, the sun and moon also experienced ritual veneration (Figs. 29, 30).

The great popularity of sun or star pendants may possibly be traceable to the ancient Near Eastern goddesses Astarte and Ishtar, both of whom are associated with the sun and stars as well as the moon. An antique statuette may be a representation of the Mesopotamian Ishtar, who is equated with Venus, with a crescent moon, its tips pointing upwards, on her head (Fig. 31).

The ancient civilisation known as Luristan existed in the Zagros Mountains, in north-western Persia, and is chiefly distinguished by the fascinating bronze objects associated with it. Under the influence of other early Near Eastern civilisations, the bronze founders of the Luristan region also created pieces of jewellery – which are highly likely to have been cult objects – with the stars as their magical content. To take just one example, a bronze finger ring from the early first millennium BC has survived. The numerous stars depicted on it probably represent the firmament, which was the object of veneration (Fig. 32).

Erhalten hat sich zum Beispiel ein bronzener Fingerring aus dem frühen 1. Jahrtausend. Die zahlreichen Sterne, die auf ihm dargestellt sind, repräsentieren wohl das Firmament, das es zu verehren galt (Abb. 32). Ein anderer Ring aus Bronze – er stammt vermutlich aus dem achämenidischen Persien des späten 6. Jahrhunderts v. Chr. – zeigt auf spitzovaler Siegelplatte einen Mann auf einem Thron. Vor ihm ist das Sternbild der Plejaden zu sehen, offenbar der Gegenstand seiner kultischen Handlung (Abb. 33). Das Siebengestirn scheint in der altorientalischen Welt eine herausragende Rolle gespielt zu haben, ist es doch auch auf anderen Schmuckstücken dieser Region immer wieder dargestellt.

Bei den nomadischen Skythen standen die Gestirne offenbar ebenfalls in einem magisch-religiösen Kontext. Das legt ein goldenes Sonnenrad aus dem 5. bis 4. Jahrhundert v. Chr. nahe, das im Zuge von Ausgrabungen in der Nekropole von Kosh-Pei in der südsibirischen Republik Tuwa gefunden wurde.[32]

Wie schon in Ägypten spielten die Gestirne offenbar auch in den orientalischen und nomadischen Kulturen der alten Welt eine maßgebliche Rolle. Schmuckstücke, die mit den magischen und mythischen Zeichen der Himmelskörper versehen sind, liefern hierfür den Beweis.

KRETA, GRIECHENLAND UND ROM

Die minoisch-mykenische Kultur, die in ihren mittleren und späten Perioden ungefähr die Zeit zwischen 2000 und 1100 v. Chr. umfasst, gilt als die erste Hochkultur Europas. Kreta, die Insel des legendären Königs Minos, war auch auf den Gebieten der Goldschmiedekunst und des Schmuckes eine wichtige Vermittlerin zwischen Ägypten beziehungsweise dem alten Orient und den sich bildenden europäischen Kulturen.

Eine nicht unbedeutende Rolle spielten hierbei die von Heinrich Schliemann gefundenen goldenen Geschmeide, die – obwohl in Mykene entdeckt – wohl auf Kreta entstanden sind. Der Einfluss südlicher und östlicher Kulturen, Religionen und Mythologien ist beispielsweise erkennbar auf einem der goldenen Fingerringe (Abb. 34). Auf seiner Siegelfläche ist eine gesellschaftlich hochstehende Dame (oder ist es eine Göttin?) in der für Kreta charakteristischen Kleidung dargestellt: unbedeckte Brüste und langer Rock. Sie bekommt von zwei Gefährtinnen

34 Siegelring mit Darstellung einer Anbetung, weiblichen Figuren, Landschaft, Sonne und Mond, Mykene, Schatz der Akropolis, mykenisch-minoisch, um 1500 v. Chr., Gold. Signet ring with worship scene, female figures, landscape, sun and moon, from Mycenae, Acropolis treasure, Minoan and Mycenean civilisations, c.1500 BC, gold. National Archaeological Museum, Athens

The pointed oval seal-bearing bezel of another bronze ring – it probably dates from the late sixth century BC and came from Achaemenid Persia – features a man on a throne. In front of him the constellation known as the Pleiades, or Seven Sisters, is depicted, evidently the object of the cult observance he is engaged in (Fig. 33). The Seven Sisters seem to have played a special role in the ancient Near East because representations of the constellation are also encountered on many other pieces of jewellery from this region.

Among the nomadic Scytheans the stars were evidently also placed in a magical religious context. A gold sun-wheel dating from the fifth to fourth centuries BC found in the course of excavations conducted at the necropolis of Kosh Pei in the southern Siberian republic of Tuva suggests that this was the case.[32]

As in ancient Egypt, the stars evidently played a paramount role in the Near Eastern and nomadic cultures of the ancient world. Pieces of jewellery bearing the magical and mythical symbols for the heavenly bodies provide evidence for this assertion.

35 Goldene Krone aus Grab III des Gräberrunds A in Mykene, mykenisch, 16. Jh. v. Chr., Gold. Gold crown from Tomb III, from the Circle A of Mycenae, Mycenaean civilisation, 16th century BC, gold. National Archaeological Museum, Athens

oder Adorantinnen Blumensträuße überreicht. Über dieser Szene stehen eine Sonnenscheibe und eine Mondsichel. Nahe verwandt und möglicherweise abgeleitet von entsprechenden Darstellungen aus den orientalischen Kulturkreisen erscheinen Sonne und Mond auch auf einem weiteren Siegelring, der von Schliemann in Tiryns, unweit der mykenischen Fundstätten, ausgegraben wurde.[33] Die Ringe werden in die Zeit zwischen 1500 und 1400 v. Chr. datiert. Bereits aus dem 16. Jahrhundert stammt zudem eine große goldene Krone, möglicherweise eine Grabbeigabe, die mit zahlreichen Sonnensymbolen geschmückt ist (Abb. 35).

Jahrhunderte später, als sich die hellenische Kultur längst ausgebildet hatte, als der politische, literarische und künstlerische Rang der griechischen Stadtstaaten und vor allem Athens in hoher Blüte stand, gewann die Sonne als Symbol des antiken Makedonien einen besonderen Rang. Die sogenannte Sonne von Vergina (gelegentlich und wohl fälschlicherweise auch als Stern von Vergina bezeichnet) war im 4. Jahrhundert v. Chr. unter Philipp II. und Alexander dem Großen zum Emblem der makedonischen Herrscherfamilie geworden. Die sechzehn Strahlen zieren beispielsweise die goldene Urne, in der die sterblichen Überreste Philipps bestattet wurden, und bezeichnen den hohen Rang des verstorbenen Herrschers.

CRETE, GREECE AND ROME

The Minoan and Mycenean civilisations, which roughly cover the timespan between 2000 and 1100 BC, are regarded as Europe's first advanced civilisations. Crete, the island of the legendary King Minos, was an important intermediary between ancient Egypt, or rather the ancient Near East, and the emerging European civilisations in the crafts of goldsmithing and jewellery-making.

The gold jewellery discovered by Heinrich Schliemann was probably made on Crete – although it was found at Mycene – and played a very important role in this connection. The influence of southern and eastern civilisations, religions and mythologies is, to take one example, discernible in one of the gold finger rings from Mycene (Fig. 34). On its seal-bearing bezel a lady of high social rank (or is she a goddess?) is depicted dressed in clothing characteristic of Crete: bare breasts and a long, flounced skirt. Two female companions or worshippers are offering bunches of flowers to her. Above this scene are a sun disc and a crescent moon. Another seal ring, dug up by Schliemann in Tiryns, which is not all that far from the site of the Mycenean finds, is closely related to, and possibly derives from, similar representations known from ancient Near Eastern civilisations.[33] These two rings are dated to between 1500 and 1400 BC. Moreover, a large gold crown, possibly from a burial, is decorated with numerous sun symbols and predates the rings as it is from the sixteenth century BC (Fig. 35).

Centuries later, when Hellenic culture had long since fully developed, when the political, literary and artistic flowering of the Greek city states, and notably Athens, was at its height, the sun was accorded special status as the symbol of ancient Macedon. The so-called Sun of Vergina (also occasionally and probably erroneously known as the Star of Vergina) was made the emblem of the Macedonian royal family under Philip II and Alexander the Great in the fourth century BC. Its sixteen rays decorate the gold larnax in which Philip's mortal remains were entombed and mark the high rank of the dead king.

A medallion-like disc from the Hellenistic period, on which the mother goddess Cybele, originally an Anatolian deity, is depicted in a chariot drawn by two lions, also features the Sun of Vergina emblem. A winged female companion of the goddess's is pointing with a staff to the sun god, Helios, in a gold aureole, who is accompanied by a gold crescent moon and a sixteen-pointed star.[34] The Vergina sun motif also appears occasionally with fewer rays – for instance, on a gold disc dating to between 350 and 325 BC.[35] There the sun has only eight rays. The number of rays is assumed to have marked the social status of the person to whom the sun emblem referred.

As the personification of the sun, Helios (son of Hyperion and Theia) played a pivotal role among the minor residents of Mount Olympus. Led by his sister Eos, the personification of the dawn, Helios spent the day moving across the sky in the sun chariot drawn by four horses (see Fig. 3). Gold ear jewellery dating from the fourth to the third century BC demonstrates that Helios and his life-giving powers were also honoured in jewellery. The countenance of the personification of the sun is framed on a golden brooch by twenty-eight rays (Fig. 36).[36] As *Sol invictus* (Latin: 'the Sun invincible') he was also venerated in

36 Brosche mit Helioskopf, 4.-3. Jh. v. Chr., Gold, Dm 3,8 cm. Brooch with the head of Helios, 4th-3rd century BC, gold, dia. 3.8 cm. Musée du Louvre, Paris, Département des Antiquités grecques, étrusques et romaines, Inv. BJ962

Auch auf einer medaillonartigen Scheibe aus hellenistischer Zeit, die die ursprünglich anatolische Muttergottheit Cybele in ihrem von zwei Löwen gezogenen Prunkwagen zeigt, ist die Sonne von Vergina zu sehen. Eine geflügelte Begleiterin der Göttin weist mit einem Stab auf den Sonnengott Helios im goldenen Strahlenkranz, der begleitet wird von einer goldenen Mondsichel und einem sechzehnstrahligen Stern.[34] Doch erscheint das Vergina-Sonnenmotiv zuweilen auch in der Version mit weniger Strahlen, etwa auf einer goldenen Scheibe, die in die Zeit zwischen 350 und 325 v. Chr. datiert wird.[35] Dort hat die Sonne nur acht Strahlen. Es wird angenommen, dass die Anzahl der Strahlen die gesellschaftliche Stellung der Persönlichkeit anzeigte, auf die sich das Sonnenzeichen bezog.

Helios, der Sohn von Hyperion und Theia, nahm als Sonnengott einen zentralen Platz in der griechischen Götterwelt ein. Angeführt von seiner Schwester Eos, der Personifikation der Morgenröte, zog er in einem vierspännigen Sonnenwagen durch den Tag (s. Abb. 3). Dass Helios und seine lebensspendende Kraft auch im Schmuck gewürdigt wurden, beweist eine goldene Brosche aus dem 4. bis 3. Jahrhundert v. Chr. Das darauf dargestellte Antlitz des Sonnengottes wird von 28 Strahlen umrahmt (Abb. 36).[36] Als *Sol invictus* (lat.: unbesiegter Sonnengott) wurde ihm auch in römischer Zeit Verehrung zuteil. Ein goldenes Medaillon mit drei Almandinen aus dem 2. Jahrhundert n. Chr. legt davon Zeugnis ab; es stammt aus dem Schatz von Gonio in Georgien.[37] Auch die Sonnengottheit Mithras mag Pate gestanden haben für die religiös motivierten Sonnenschmuckstücke, die in Rom und allen Teilen des Imperiums populär waren. Der ursprünglich aus Persien stammende Kult erreichte hier im 2. und 3. Jahrhundert n. Chr. seinen Höhepunkt.

Symbol der griechischen Göttin Selene – und später der römischen Luna – war die Mondsichel. In dem wohl berühmtesten Schmuckzentrum der hellenistischen

37 Lunula-Anhänger, nabatäisch-hellenistisch, 2. Jh. v. Chr., Gold, Granate, 4,5 × 5 cm. Lunula pendant, Nabatean-Hellenistic, 2nd century BC, gold, garnets, 4.5 × 5 cm. Schmuckmuseum Pforzheim

Roman times. A gold medallion (second century AD) set with three almandine garnets bears witness to the cult; it came from the Gonio Treasure found in Georgia.[37] The sun god Mithras may also have been the model for the devotionally motivated pieces of sun jewellery that were so popular in Rome and all parts of the Roman Empire. The Mithraic cult, which originally came from Persia, reached its acme here in the second and third centuries AD.

The crescent moon was the symbol of the Greek goddess Selene – and later of Luna, her Roman counterpart. A pendant in the form of a crescent moon with rich filigree decoration was made at Tarentum in Magna Graecia, probably the most famous jewellery-making centre in the Hellenistic period.[38] A Nabataean Hellenistic piece of moon jewellery with cabochon garnets and delicate filigree decoration has also survived (Fig. 37). In Roman times the crescent moon became a popular jewellery motif, to which apotropaic powers must surely have been imputed.

What is certain is that the lunula was worn as a pendant wherever the Mithraic cult spread – and it was worn by both men and women. Whether in Palmyra (where numerous funereal busts from the second and third centuries AD attest to the moon pendant[39]), Asia Minor (Fig. 38) or north of the Alps (for instance, in the Rhineland or southern Germany), Luna has been verifiably associated with many Roman pieces of jewellery. Mummy portraits in Hawara, Faiyum, attest to

38 Lunula-Anhänger, Kleinasien, 1.–2. Jh. n. Chr., Gold, H 2,6 cm. Lunula pendant, Asia Minor, 1st–2nd century AD, H 2.6 cm. Archäologische Staatssammlung München, Inv. 1975,369

Zeit, dem großgriechischen Tarent, wurde ein reich mit Filigran verzierter Anhänger in Mondsichelform geschaffen.[38] Auch ein nabatäisch-hellenistisches Schmuckstück mit Granatcabochons und feiner Filigranverzierung hat sich erhalten (Abb. 37). In römischer Zeit wurde die Mondsichel zu einem beliebten Schmuckmotiv, dem man sicherlich apotropäische Eigenschaften zusprach.

Mit Sicherheit kann man festhalten, dass die Lunula als Anhänger überall dort getragen wurde, wo sich der Mithras-Kult ausgebreitet hatte – und zwar von Männern ebenso wie von Frauen. Ob in Palmyra (dort ist der Mondanhänger zusammen mit anderen Schmuckstücken auf zahlreichen Grabbüsten aus dem 2. und 3. Jahrhundert n. Chr. bezeugt[39]), in Kleinasien (Abb. 38) oder im nordalpinen Raum (etwa im Rheinland oder in Süddeutschland): Luna ist in römischen Schmuckstücken vielfältig nachweisbar. Mumienporträts aus Hawara, Fayum, beweisen die Beliebtheit und die weite Verbreitung der Mondsichelanhänger auch für den ägyptischen Raum (Abb. 39).[40] Doch sind bereits aus sehr viel früherer Zeit, aus Sumer beispielsweise, entsprechende Anhänger dokumentiert. Der weiter oben erwähnte Dilbat-Halsschmuck etwa trägt zusammen mit den drei Sonnenscheiben eine granulierte Mondsichel (s. S. 50).

39 Mumienporträt einer Dame mit Goldohrringen und Lunula-Anhänger, Hawara, Fayum, Ägypten, römische Kaiserzeit, um 70 n. Chr., Enkaustik auf Holz, 32,5 × 21,8 cm. Mummy portrait of a lady with gold earrings and a lunula pendant, from Hawara, Faiyum, Egypt, Roman Empire, *c.*70 AD, encaustic on wood, 32.5 × 21.8 cm. Ägyptisches Museum und Papyrussammlung, Staatliche Museen zu Berlin – Preußischer Kulturbesitz, Inv. ÄM 10974

40 Mumienporträt eines Priesters des Serapis, Hawara, Fayum, Ägypten, 140–160 n. Chr., Enkaustik auf Lindenholz, 42,5 × 22,2 cm. Mummy portrait of a priest of Serapis's, from Hawara, Faiyum, Egypt, c.140–160 AD, encaustic on lime wood, 42.5 × 22.2 cm. British Museum, London, Inv. 1994,0521.12 74714

Die Darstellung der römischen Mondgöttin Diana auf dem Intaglio eines römischen Ringes aus dem 3. Jahrhundert n. Chr. folgt dem Typus der Artemis Ephesia. Sie ist flankiert von einem Stern und einer Mondsichel, was diese Himmelkörper auch hier eindeutig in den mythologisch-religiösen Bereich hebt (Abb. 42). Das gilt in anderer Weise – nun bezogen auf den Stern als kultisch-magisches Abbild – auch für das Mumienbildnis eines bärtigen Mannes aus Hawara in Ägypten, das in das 2. Jahrhundert n. Chr. datiert wird. Er trägt ein goldenes Stirnband mit einem siebenstrahligen Stern. Vermutlich war der Dargestellte ein Priester oder hoher Beamter des in frühhellenistischer Zeit in Ägypten entstandenen Serapis-Kultes, in dem sich griechische und ägyptische Traditionen verbanden (Abb. 40).

Eine Bronzebrosche mit dem stilisierten Sonnenmotiv der Swastika[41] schließlich ist wohl keltisch-römischer Herkunft und beweist, dass die Sonne in dieser abstrahierten Form – wohl weniger häufig als die Mondsichel – auch in dem von den Römern beeinflussten nordalpinen Raum als Zeichen und Motiv für Schmuckstücke gedient hat.

41 Sonnenscheibe von Moordorf, gefunden in Moordorf (Ostfriesland), Bronzezeit, 1800–750 v. Chr., Gold, Dm 14,5 cm. Moordorf sun disc, found in Moordorf (Eastern Friesland), Bronze Age, 1800–750 BC, gold, dia. 14.5 cm. Niedersächsisches Landesmuseum, Hannover

42 Ring mit Darstellung der Mondgöttin Diana, römisch, 3. Jh. n. Chr., Gold, Karneol. Ring depicting Diana, the goddess of the moon, Roman, 3rd century BC, gold, carnelian. Museum für Angewandte Kunst Köln, Inv. G 1132

Aus dem nordalpinen Raum hat sich aus der frühen Eisenzeit auch die sogenannte Sonnenscheibe von Moordorf erhalten. Sie zeigt eine von 32 dreieckigen Strahlen umrahmte Sonne (Abb. 41) und dürfte wohl im Zusammenhang mit der Goldschale von Zürich-Altstetten, den goldenen Hüten von Schifferstadt und Etzelsdorf sowie dem Goldhut in Berlin in Zusammenhang stehen (s. S. 36). Ein goldener Zermonial-Halskragen, der wohl aus dem Ostalpenraum stammt und in das 10. bis 9. Jahrhundert datiert werden kann, bezeugt, dass auch dort kultisch genutzte Schmuckstücke mit dem Sonnenmotiv ausgestattet worden sind.[42]

Dass in allen genannten Fällen apotropäische, religiöse und magisch-mythische Beweggründe vor den rein schmückenden Belangen standen, mag wohl außer Zweifel stehen.

ETRURIEN

In Mittelitalien, in der heutigen Toskana, in Umbrien und im Latium, lebten seit der Zeit um 800 v. Chr. die Etrusker, deren Herkunft die Wissenschaft bis heute noch nicht endgültig klären konnte. In Religion und Mythologie, Kunst und Handwerk waren sie von anderen mittelmeerischen Kulturen beeinflusst. So spricht man zum Beispiel von einer orientalisierenden Periode, auch existierten vielfältige Beziehungen zur hellenischen Kultur. Dennoch entwickelten die Etrusker auf anderen Gebieten durchaus eigenständige Vorstellungen und Werte.[43] Und unbestreitbar ist: In der Goldschmiedekunst leisteten die Etrusker Außergewöhnliches. Besonders im 7. und 6. Jahrhundert v. Chr. erreichten sie auf diesem Gebiet höchstes Niveau.

Die Granulation, eine der feinsten und raffiniertesten Goldschmiedetechniken überhaupt, beherrschten die Etrusker meisterhaft. Kleinste goldene Kügelchen, die sogenannten Granalien, wurden dabei mit einem metallischen Untergrund verschweißt – zur Verzierung der Goldschmiedearbeiten sowohl mit figürlichem als auch mit geometrischem Dekor. Zwar erfanden die etruskischen Goldschmiede die Granulation nicht eigenständig – sie war bereits im 2. Jahrtausend v. Chr. in Ägypten und in Sumer angewendet worden – doch brachten sie sie zu einer nie zuvor und später nur selten erreichten Blüte.[44]

Es wird vermutet, dass die Etrusker einen Sonnengott verehrten, dem sie den Namen Usil gegeben hatten. Tivr war wohl ein männlicher Mondgott, während Lusna, möglicherweise verwandt mit der römischen Luna, eine Mondgöttin gewesen zu sein scheint. Es ist deshalb naheliegend, die etruskischen Schmuckstücke, auf denen Sonne und Mond abgebildet sind, mit den Gestirnen in magischem Zusammenhang zu sehen. So auch im Falle der zentralen Scheibe eines Halsschmucks aus dem letzten Viertel des 7. Jahrhunderts, auf der – mit Granulation

the popularity and wide dissemination of the crescent moon pendant in Roman Egypt, too (Fig. 39).⁴⁰ Similar pendants are, however, recorded from far earlier times, from Sumer, for instance. The Dilbat neck jewellery mentioned above features a granulated crescent moon along with its three sun discs (see p. 53).

A representation of Diana, the Roman goddess of the moon, on an intaglio in a ring dating from the third century AD is of the Artemis Ephesia type. Flanked by a star and a crescent moon, the Roman goddess unambiguously elevates these heavenly bodies to the mythological-religious plane (Fig. 42). This is also true in a different way – now in relation to the star as a magical cult image – of a mummy portrait of a bearded man from Hawara in Egypt (second century AD). He is depicted wearing a golden headband with a seven-pointed star. The man whose portrait this is was probably a priest or a high-ranking official associated with the syncretistic Serapis cult linking Greek and Egyptian traditions that emerged in Egypt in the early Hellenistic period (Fig. 40).

Finally, a bronze brooch with the stylised sun motif in the form of a swastika⁴¹ is probably of Romano-Celtic origin. It proves that the sun in this abstract form – probably less frequently than the crescent moon – was also used as a sign and motif for jewellery in regions under the sway of the Romans north of the Alps.

The early Iron Age artefact known as the Moordorf sun disc is also from north of the Alps. On it a sun framed by thirty-two triangular rays is depicted (Fig. 41). The Moordorf sun disc is probably associated with the gold bowl from Zurich-Altstetten, the tall gold 'hats' from Schifferstadt and Etzelsdorf and the gold hat in Berlin (see p. 39). A gold ceremonial collar, which likely originates from east of the Alps and can be dated to the tenth to ninth centuries, attests that there, too, jewellery pieces used in rituals had been invested with the sun motif.⁴²

Beyond all doubt, therefore, apotropaic, religious and magical-mythical motives had priority over considerations related purely to adornment in all the above cases.

ETRURIA
From about 800 BC the Etruscans lived in central Italy in the areas now known as Tuscany, Umbria and Lazio. The origins of this people have yet to be unequivocally clarified by scholars; in religion and mythology, art and crafts they were influenced by other Mediterranean cultures. An orientalising period is mentioned in connection with Etruscan art, for example, and there are numerous links to Hellenic civilisation. Nonetheless, the Etruscans developed markedly independent ideas and values in other areas.⁴³ And what the Etruscans achieved as goldsmiths was by any measure extraordinary. In the seventh and sixth centuries BC especially they attained the highest standard in this field.

The Etruscans were past masters at granulation, one of the finest and most sophisticated goldsmithing techniques ever invented. Minuscule gold balls, known as granules, were attached to a metallic surface by means of reaction soldering and sintering in order to embellish jewellery made by goldsmiths with both figurative and geometric decoration. True, the Etruscans were not the inventors of granulation – it had already been used as long ago as the second

43 Halsschmuck, Vulci, Etrurien, letztes Viertel 7. Jh. v. Chr., Gold, L 26,3 cm. Necklace, Vulci, Etruria, latter quarter of the 7th century BC, gold, L 26.3 cm. Staatliche Antikensammlungen München, Inv. 2339

verziert – sowohl die Sonne als auch die Mondsichel zu sehen sind (Abb. 43). Ein im späten 8. Jahrhundert entstandener Halsschmuck besteht aus fünf goldenen Scheiben, die ebenfalls jeweils eine Sonne und eine Mondsichel zeigen.[45] Und die reich mit Granulation verzierten goldenen Ohrscheiben, auf denen jede einzelne Granalie die Strahlen der realen Sonne widerspiegeln konnte, dürfen als Symbole und Abbilder der Sonne betrachtet werden (Abb. 44).

Die Bewohner der zwölf etruskischen Städte waren – wie vor allem aus römischen Quellen bekannt ist – tief religiös; die von den priesterlichen Haruspices praktizierte Leberbeschau zur Bestimmung in der Zukunft liegender Ereignisse unterstreicht dies nachdrücklich. Dass die Etrusker auch an Einflüsse aus dem Universum geglaubt haben, lässt sich erahnen, wenn die großartigen Werke etruskischer Goldschmiedekunst in die Betrachtung miteinbezogen werden.

Schon aus der voretruskischen Zeit Mittelitaliens sind große goldene Sonnenscheiben bezeugt. Ein Beispiel aus dem 8. Jahrhundert v. Chr. zeigt eine Dreiergruppe, die mit Bernsteinperlen zu einem Halsschmuck gefügt sind (Abb. 45).

44 Zierscheiben, etruskisch, 6. Jh. v. Chr., Gold mit Granulation, Dm 4,5 cm.
Decorative discs, Etruscan, 6th century BC, gold with granulation, dia. 4.5 cm.
Schmuckmuseum Pforzheim, Inv. 1969/116

45 Halsschmuck, gefunden in Bisenzio (Toskana), Italien, etruskisch, 8. Jh. v. Chr., Gold, Bernsteinperlen. Necklace, found in Bisenzio (Tuscany), Italy, Etruscan, 8th century BC, gold, amber beads. Museo Nazionale Etrusco di Villa Giulia, Roma

VÖLKERWANDERUNGSZEIT, MITTELALTER UND RENAISSANCE

Ob und in welchem Umfang in der Völkerwanderungszeit, im Mittelalter und in der Renaissance die Gestirne als Schmuckmotive gedient haben, darüber ist nur wenig bekannt. In einem süddeutschen Grab des frühen 8. Jahrhunderts n. Chr. wurde eine sternförmige goldene, mit Almandinen verzierte Fibel gefunden (Abb. 46). Eine vermutlich der oberen Gesellschaftsschicht angehörende Dame war darin bestattet worden. Zusammen mit einer ins 7. Jahrhundert datierten filigranverzierten Goldscheibe aus dem langobardischen Italien und einer fränkischen Goldscheibenfibel[46] aus dem 7. oder 8. Jahrhundert gehört sie zu den wenigen bisher bekannten Sternschmuckstücken des frühen Mittelalters. Auch eine vermutlich um 600 n. Chr. entstandene schwere goldene Kette ist bekannt. Einige Jahrzehnte vor der

46 Goldscheibenfibel in Form eines achtzackigen Sternes, gefunden in Fridingen, Kreis Tuttlingen, Grab 278, frühes 8. Jh., Gold, Almandine. Gold disc fibula in the shape of an eight-sided star, found in Fridingen, district of Tuttlingen, Tomb 278, early 8th century, gold, almandines. Landesmuseum Württemberg, Stuttgart, Inv. F 85,236-1

millennium BC in Egypt and Sumer – yet they were the ones to take it to the heights of an unprecedented heyday that would only rarely be matched later.[44]

The Etruscans are believed to have venerated a sun god, whom they called Usil. Tivr was probably a male moon deity whereas Lusna, possibly related to the Roman Luna, seems to have been a moon goddess. It would seem obvious, therefore, that pieces of Etruscan jewellery on which the sun and moon are represented should be viewed as being in a magical context with the heavenly bodies. This is the case with the central disc of a piece of neck jewellery dating from the last quarter of the seventh century on which – decorated with granulation – both the sun and the crescent moon are to be seen (Fig. 43). A piece of neck jewellery made in the late eighth century consists of five gold discs, each displaying a sun and a crescent moon.[45] And gold ear discs, so richly decorated with granulation that every single granule could reflect the rays of the real sun, can be viewed as symbols and images of the sun (Fig. 44).

The inhabitants of the twelve Etruscan towns were – as is known from sources, most of which are Roman – deeply religious. This inference is compellingly underscored by the fact that priestly haruspices practised divination by hepatoscopy – that is, examining the liver of sacrificial animals to ascertain the outcomes of future events. When the superb works by Etruscan goldsmiths are taken into consideration as well, some idea is conveyed of how the Etruscans must also have believed in cosmic influences.

Large gold sun discs are extant from even pre-Etruscan central Italy. One example from the eighth century BC features a triad that has been fitted together with amber beads to make a necklace (Fig. 45).

THE MIGRATION PERIOD, THE MIDDLE AGES, AND THE RENAISSANCE

Not much is known about whether and to what extent the sun, moon and stars were used as jewellery motifs in the Migration period, the Middle Ages, and the Renaissance. A south German grave from the early eighth century AD yielded a star-shaped gold fibula set with almandine garnets (Fig. 46). A lady who presumably belonged to the upper class was buried in the grave. Along with a filigree-embellished gold disc from Lombardy dated to the seventh century and a Frankish disc brooch from the seventh or eighth century decorated with filigree,[46] the south German gold fibula set with garnets is one of only a handful of early medieval star-shaped pieces of jewellery known. A heavy gold chain presumed to date from about AD 600 is also extant. It was probably made in a Syrian monastery under Byzantine influence just a few decades before Islam was founded by the

47 Lunula-Anhänger an Kette, Syrien, byzantinisch, um 600 n. Chr., Gold, Sardonyx, Smaragde, Saphir, Perlen, B 5,4 cm. Lunula pendant on a chain, Syria, Byzantine, *c.*1600 BC, gold, sardonyx, emeralds, sapphire, pearls, W 5.4 cm.
Schmuckmuseum Pforzheim, Leihgabe / on permanent loan from the Ministerium für Wissenschaft, Forschung und Kunst Baden-Württemberg, Inv. LBW 1971-1

48 Anhänger mit Madonna auf der Mondsichel, Deutschland, um 1510, Silber, teilweise vergoldet, Dm 9 cm.
Pendant with Virgin and Child on a crescent moon, Germany, c.1510, parcel-gilt silver, dia. 9 cm. KHM-Museumsverband, Wien, Inv. KK 9024

49 Albrecht Dürer, *Madonna auf der Mondsichel*, Titelblatt des *Marienlebens*, um 1510, Holzschnitt. Albrecht Dürer, *Virgin and Child on a Crescent Moon*, frontispiece of *Marienleben*, c.1510, woodcut. Kupferstichkabinett, Staatliche Museen zu Berlin - Preußischer Kulturbesitz, Inv. 140-2

Prophet Mohammad. Set with precious stones, the lunula pendant on the chain in the ancient Near Eastern tradition alludes to Ishtar or Selene (Fig. 47). From the third to the eleventh centuries there were granulated crescent moon pendants in gold and silver – revealing both Byzantine and Islamic stylistic influence and presumably also similarly syncretistic religious thinking – in Russia and some other eastern European regions.[47] Late medieval finger rings with crescent-moon and star motifs, most of them from eastern and south-eastern Europe, should probably be viewed as associated with the lower echelons of the aristocracy in Hungary and Poland, who had moons and stars as heraldic devices.[48]

The next piece of jewellery that may have possibly used the star motif is several centuries younger: a *spilla* (pin), lavishly decorated with precious stones and pearls, is dated to the mid-fourteenth century. Specialist publications call it a *Spilla a stella* or *Sternbrosche* [German: star brooch] although it might well be a stylised flower with twelve petals.[49]

A silver-gilt pendant with the Madonna, crowned and in an aureole, and Child was probably made in southern Germany c.1510. A half-figure representation, the Virgin is holding her child in her arms and is on a crescent moon – as in Albrecht Dürer's work of the same time (Figs. 48, 49). Around the year 1515 the Swabian painter Bernhard Strigel (celebrated for a group portrait of the lavishly bejewelled Emperor Maximilian I and his family) painted the portrait

Gründung des Islam durch den Propheten Mohammed wurde sie wohl in einem syrischen Kloster unter byzantinischem Einfluss geschaffen. Der edelsteinbesetze Lunula-Anhänger in antik-orientalischer Tradition verweist auf Ishtar oder Selene (Abb. 47). Granulierte Mondsichelanhänger aus Gold und Silber gab es – vermutlich unter byzantinischem sowie islamischem und damit auch religiösem Einfluss – vom 3. bis 11. Jahrhundert in Russland und manch anderen osteuropäischen Regionen.[47] Spätmittelalterliche Fingerringe mit Mondsichel- und Sternmotiven, vornehmlich aus Ost- und Südosteuropa, sind wohl in Zusammenhang zu sehen mit niedrigen Adelsgeschlechtern in Ungarn und Polen, deren heraldische Zeichen Monde und Sterne gewesen sind.[48]

Erst einige Jahrhunderte später findet sich ein weiteres Schmuckstück, das sich möglicherweise der Sternenmotivik bedient: Eine reich mit Edelsteinen und Perlen geschmückte *spilla* wird auf die Mitte des 14. Jahrhunderts datiert. In der Literatur ist sie mit dem Namen *Spilla a stella* beziehungsweise *Sternbrosche* bezeichnet; es könnte sich aber auch um eine zwölfblättrige Blüte handeln.[49]

Vermutlich in Süddeutschland entstand um 1510 ein silbervergoldeter Anhänger, der eine bekrönte Madonna im Strahlenkranz zeigt. Als Halbfigur dargestellt, hält sie ihr Kind in den Armen und wird – wie etwa bei Albrecht Dürer zur gleichen Zeit – von der Mondsichel unterfangen (Abb. 48, 49). Um das Jahr 1515 porträtierte der schwäbische Maler Bernhard Strigel (berühmt geworden mit einem Bildnis der reich geschmückten Familie Kaiser Maximilians I.) die einer wohlhabenden Augsburger Familie angehörende Sibylla von Freyberg (Abb. 50). Neben vielen Ketten, Fingerringen und anderen Preziosen trägt sie einen Anhänger, der in Ableitung des apokalyptischen Weibes aus der Offenbarung des Johannes das Motiv der sogenannten Mondsichelmadonna zeigt (s. S. 18). Der Anhänger ist Bestandteil der Insignie des 1440 durch Kurfürst Friedrich II. von Brandenburg gestifteten Schwanenordens (Orden unserer lieben Frauen zum Schwan), dem auch vornehme Damen angehörten. Trotz anderer Anordnung einzelner Details – Maria hält bei Dürer das Kind auf der anderen Seite als auf dem Schmuckstück und die goldenen Strahlen sind hier nach unten gerichtet – entsprechen sowohl der Anhänger als auch die Ordensinsignie der im späten Mittelalter gültigen Ikonografie: ein Beweis dafür, dass die Schmuckkunst im 16. Jahrhundert – neben vielen profanen Motiven – gelegentlich auch noch einen religiösen Aspekt aufweist.

Auch auf einem Bildnis, das möglicherweise zu Beginn des 16. Jahrhunderts von dem fränkischen Maler Sebald Bopp geschaffen wurde, erscheinen die Insignien des Schwanenordens mit dem Anhänger der sonnenumstrahlten, auf einer Mondsichel ruhenden Muttergottes. Das Bild ist der heiligen Hemma von Gurk gewidmet und stellt vermutlich Beatrix von Frangepan dar, die Gemahlin Georgs von Brandenburg-Ansbach.

50 Bernhard Strigel, *Sibylla von Freyberg, geb. Gossenbrot* (Detail), um 1515, Öl auf Lindenholz, 61 × 35,8 cm. Bernhard Strigel, *Sibylla von Freyberg, née Gossenbrot* (detail), c.1515, oil on lime wood, 61 × 35,8 cm. Bayerische Staatsgemäldesammlungen – Alte Pinakothek, München, Inv. 9347

Als besonders interessantes Beispiel eines Sonnenschmuckstücks aus dem 16. Jahrhundert gilt ein Anhänger des Sklavenhändlers, Piraten, Weltumseglers und Eroberers Sir Francis Drake. Das sogenannte *Sun Jewel* trägt, umgeben von einem Strahlenkranz, auf der einen Seite ein Miniaturbildnis der englischen Königin Elisabeth I. (Drake hatte das Schmuckstück 1590 von ihr als Neujahrsgeschenk erhalten). Die andere Seite ist reich mit Rubinen und Opalen ausgefasst und wird in der Mitte von einem Siegel-Rubin-Intaglio der Königin dominiert.[50] Würdigt die Monarchin mit dem Sonnensymbol und ihrem eigenen Porträt die Erfolge, die Drake rund um den Globus – der Sonne gleich – für das Königreich erzielt hat?

Religiöse und weltliche Beweggründe haben über Jahrhunderte dazu geführt, dass die Gestirne – den jeweiligen gesellschaftlichen und politischen Gegebenheiten entsprechend – ihren Platz in der Gestaltung von Schmuck behalten haben. Tiefgreifende Umbruchzeiten mit revolutionären Ideen spielten dabei ebenso eine Rolle wie konservative Aspekte des Bewahrens.

BAROCKZEIT

Im Barock beginnt eine Hoch-Zeit in der Auseinandersetzung mit den Gestirnen, die bis zum heutigen Tage anhält: Astronomie und Astrologie feiern Triumphe. Was die Wissenschaft im 16. und 17. Jahrhundert an Neuem herausfand, was Nikolaus Kopernikus, Tycho Brahe, Johannes Kepler und andere Forscher entdeckten und beschrieben, schlägt sich vielfältig in den Künsten und im Kunsthandwerk nieder.

Auch die sogenannten großen Kometen, nicht zuletzt der alle 75 bis 76 Jahre erscheinende Halleysche Komet, wurden immer wieder von Künstlern dargestellt.[51] Geschäftstüchtige Juweliere und Goldschmiede nahmen Kometenerscheinungen gelegentlich zum Anlass, Broschen, Anhänger und Kopfschmuckstücke mit Sternmotiven zu schaffen. Herausragend und – weil vermutlich einzigartig – ist in diesem Zusammenhang ein um 1760 entstandenes Ensemble von drei zusammengehörenden Schmuckstücken: Eine Sonnen- und eine Mondagraffe sowie eine Brosche, die einen rasenden Kometen darstellt, wurden als Perückenschmuck im künstlichen, hoch aufgetürmten Haar von einer Rokoko-Dame getragen. Sie zeugen von der Begeisterung, die von den mythenbehafteten Gestirnen auch noch in einer Welt der frühen Aufklärung ausging.[52]

Es ist bemerkenswert, dass der Bruststern von Ordensinsignien ab dem 18. Jahrhundert einen wahren Siegeszug angetreten hat. Als schmückendes und ehrendes Accessoire zierte und ziert er die Brust von in doppeltem Sinne ausgezeichneten Persönlichkeiten. Frauen und Männer trugen und tragen ihn mit Stolz

of Sibylla von Freyberg, who was a member of a rich Augsburg family (Fig. 50). Along with a host of chains, finger rings and other precious adornments, she is wearing a pendant that also bears the motif – taken from the apocalyptic female from the Book of Revelation – of the so-called Madonna on the Crescent Moon (see p. 19). The pendant is an element of the insignia of the Order of the Swan formed in 1440 by Friedrich II, Elector of Brandenburg, to which ladies of high rank also belonged. Although individual details are differently arranged – in Dürer the Virgin is holding the Child on her other side and the gold rays are directed downwards here – both the pendant and the insignia of the order match the standard late medieval iconography: conclusive proof that in the sixteenth century jewellery occasionally also reveals a religious aspect – alongside many profane motifs.

The insignia of the Order of the Swan featuring the pendant with the Virgin surrounded by the rays of the sun and resting on a crescent moon also appears on a portrait that may have been painted by the Franconian painter Sebald Bopp in the early sixteenth century. Dedicated to Saint Hemma of Gurk, the portrait is believed to be a likeness of Beatrix von Frangepan, wife of Georg of Brandenburg-Ansbach.

A pendant once owned by Sir Francis Drake, slaver, pirate, circumnavigator of the globe and conqueror, is a particularly interesting example of sixteenth-century sun jewellery. Known as the *Drake Star* or the *Sun Jewel*, the pendant bears a miniature bust portrait of Elizabeth I, his sovereign, surrounded by a glory (Drake was given this jewel by the Queen as a New Year's present in 1590). The other side is sumptuously set with rubies and opals, dominated by a ruby intaglio seal that may have been the Queen's.[50] Was the monarch honouring the successes Drake had achieved for her kingdom by sailing around the world – like the sun – with the sun symbol and her own portrait?

For centuries religious and profane motives led to the heavenly bodies – corresponding in each case to social and political circumstances – retaining their place in the design of jewellery. Periods fraught with severe upheavals and underpinned by revolutionary ideas played just as much a role in ensuring the survival of this iconography as conservative aspects of preserving the status quo did.

THE BAROQUE ERA

The Baroque era ushered in the heyday of studying the heavenly bodies both scientifically and from the esoteric standpoint, a dual approach that has persisted to the present day: both astronomy and astrology were triumphant. The discoveries made by science in the sixteenth and seventeenth centuries, what Nicholas Copernicus, Tycho Brahe, Johannes Kepler and other scientists found out and wrote about, were distilled in manifold ways into both the fine and the applied arts.

Even the comets known as the great ones, not least among them Halley's Comet, which appears every seventy-five to seventy-six years, were frequently

51 Türkischer Orden, undatiert, Metall, Email, vergoldeter Halbmond. Turkish order, undated, metal, enamel, gilt crescent. Schmuckmuseum Pforzheim, Inv. 1965/14

52 Fidelitas-Orden, Stern des Hausordens der Treue, Karlsruhe, um 1900, Silber, teilvergoldet, Email. Fidelity order, Star of the House Order of Loyalty, Karlsruhe, c.1900, parcel-gilt silver, enamel. Badisches Landesmuseum Karlsruhe, Inv. MK 5481-1

und Freude vor allem im 18. und 19., aber auch noch im 20. und 21. Jahrhundert – manchmal sogar mehrere Exemplare neben- und übereinander (Abb. 51–53).

Ursprünglich mit Gold- und Silberfäden auf das Kleid oder den Uniformrock aufgestickt, entwickelte sich der Bruststern zu einem von Goldschmieden – und später von dafür ausgestatteten und lizensierten Manufakturen – geschaffenen Kleinod. Ein frühes Beispiel ist der von August dem Starken 1705 gestiftete Stern des Polnischen Weißen Adlerordens aus der sogenannten Rubin-Garnitur; er wurde zwischen 1722 und 1733 gefertigt (Abb. 54). Nur wenige Jahrzehnte später entstand der Badge of the Noble Order of Bucks; er kann auf die Zeit um 1770 datiert werden (Abb. 55). Die Gestaltung der Bruststerne mit den Insignien des jeweiligen Ordens war vielfältig und abwechslungsreich. Oft waren sie aus den wertvollsten Materialien gefertigt. Admiral Lord Nelson beispielsweise wurde vom osmanischen Sultan Selim III. der Orden des Halben Mondes verliehen, ein reich mit Diamanten besetzter Stern. Je nach Bedeutung und Rang konnten die Bruststerne aber auch aus einfachen Werkstoffen bestehen.

53   Lemuel Francis Abbott, *Konteradmiral Sir Horatio Nelson*, 1800, Öl auf Leinwand, 76,2 × 63,5 cm. Lemuel Francis Abbott, *Rear-Admiral Sir Horatio Nelson*, 1800, oil on canvas, 76.2 × 63.5 cm. National Maritime Museum, Greenwich, London, Greenwich Hospital Collection

the subject of artists' work.[51] Commercially-minded jewellers and goldsmiths occasionally chose the appearance of comets as a welcome pretext for making brooches, pendants and head jewellery with star motifs. An outstanding – because it is probably unique – example in this connection is a three-piece set (c.1760) of jewels that belong together: a sun and a moon clasp and a brooch representing a comet speeding through the sky were worn as wig jewellery by a Rococo lady, whose hairstyle would have been combed to towering heights. The pieces attest to the enthusiasm still inspired by the myth-freighted heavenly bodies even in the Age of Enlightenment.[52]

54 Johann Heinrich Köhler zugeschrieben, Bruststern des Polnischen Weißen Adler-Ordens aus der Rubingarnitur, 1722/1733, Rubine, Brillanten, Gold, Silber, teilweise vergoldet, 15,7 × 15,2 cm. Attributed to Johann Heinrich Köhler, breast star from the ruby set of the Polish Order of the White Eagle, 1722/1733, rubies, brilliant-cut diamonds, gold, silver, parcel-gilt silver, 15.7 × 15.2 cm. Staatliche Kunstsammlungen Dresden, Inv. VIII 121

55 Abzeichen des Noble Order of Bucks, England, um 1770, Silber, Glas, Email, Kupfer, Dm 8,1 cm. Badge of the Noble Order of Bucks, England, c.1770, silver, glass, enamel, copper, dia. 8.1 cm. British Museum, London, Inv. 1978,1002.72.b

56 Astronomischer Faltring, Deutschland (?), 1. Hälfte 17.Jh., Silber vergoldet. Astronomical Gemma ring, Germany (?), early half of the 17th century, silver-gilt. Schmuckmuseum Pforzheim, Inv. 1954/89

It is remarkable indeed that, from the eighteenth century on, the star triumphed as part of the insignia designating membership of an order. As a decorative accessory honouring the wearer, the star has adorned the breasts of persons distinguished in both senses of the word. Men and women have worn it with pride and joy, especially in the eighteenth and nineteenth centuries, and have continued to do so even in the twentieth and twenty-first centuries – sometimes displaying several decorations at once, juxtaposed and superimposed (Figs. 51-53).

Originally embroidered in gold and silver thread on the dress or uniform coat of the wearer, the breast star evolved into a treasure created by goldsmiths – and later produced by manufacturers specially equipped and licensed to make such badges of honours. An early example is the Star of the Polish Order of the White Eagle from what is known as the Ruby Garniture instituted by Augustus the Strong, Elector of Saxony and King of Poland, in 1705; it was made between 1722 and 1733 (Fig. 54). The badge of the Most Ancient and Honourable Society of Bucks was made only a few years later; it dates to about 1770 (Fig. 55). A wide and diverse range of design possibilities was available for breast stars of any order. They were often made of the most valuable materials. Sultan Selim III of the Ottoman Empire awarded the chivalric Order of the Crescent, a starburst lavishly set with diamonds, to Admiral Nelson. Depending on the recipient's importance and rank, a breast star might, on the other hand, also be made of simple materials.

It was not just the star motif but the entire cosmos – as represented by Albrecht Dürer in his *Armillary Spheres* woodcuts two centuries before in 1525 – that was taken up by goldsmiths. Finger rings known as astronomical rings,

57 Johann Gottlieb Scharff, Tabakdose mit Medaillon, St. Petersburg, 1780er, Gold, Silber, Labradorit, Glas, Email; getrieben, graviert, guillochiert, 3,3 × 7,4 × 5,3 cm. Johann Gottlieb Scharff, snuff box with medallion, St Petersburg, 1780s, gold, silver, labradorite, glass, enamel; chased, engraved, guilloched, 3.3 × 7.4 × 5.3 cm. The State Hermitage Museum, St Petersburg, Inv. Э-4457

Doch nicht nur das Sternmotiv, der ganze Kosmos – wie ihn schon Albrecht Dürer 1525 in seinem *Armillarsphären*-Blatt dargestellt hatte – fand Eingang in die Goldschmiedekunst. Sogenannte astronomische Ringe, die – auseinandergefaltet – das Universum darstellen (Abb. 56), waren während der Barockzeit aktuell. Aber auch andere Objekte wurden mit kosmischen Motiven ausgestattet. Ein besonders prächtiges Beispiel ist der Deckel einer runden Tabakdose, auf dem Diamanten die Umlaufbahnen der Planeten nachzeichnen. Sie wurde in den Achtzigerjahren des 18. Jahrhunderts von dem aus Deutschland stammenden Goldschmied Johann Gottlieb Scharff geschaffen, der in Sankt Petersburg für Katharina II. tätig war (Abb. 57). Ebenfalls spektakulär ist die Unterseite einer ovalen Dose, die im späten 18. Jahrhundert in Wien entstanden ist. Sie zeigt – durch Edelsteine symbolisiert – die zwölf Monate des Jahres, gehalten von den diamantbesetzten Strahlen der Sonne (Abb. 58).

Die im Barock vorherrschende Üppigkeit, in der sich die adeligen Familien und die hohe Geistlichkeit bewegten, fand ihren Niederschlag auch in den Kostbarkeiten der Goldschmiedekunst. Noch stärker als zuvor waren die Sonne, der Mond und die Sterne Motive, mit denen sich ausdrucksvoll und in repräsentativem Rahmen die hohen Ansprüche der Gesellschaft aufzeigen ließen – wohl auch wegen des gestiegenen Interesses an astronomischen und kosmologischen Fragen.

58 Tabakdose (Unterseite), Vyborg oder Wien, 1790er, Gold, Silber, Edelsteine, Ziersteine; getrieben, poliert.
Snuff box (bottom side), Vyborg or Vienna, 1790s, gold, silver, precious and decorative stones; chased, polished.
The State Hermitage Museum, St Petersburg, Inv. Э-4165

which when unfolded represented the universe (Fig. 56), were still state-of-the-art in the Baroque era. But other objects were also furnished with cosmic motifs. A particularly magnificent example is the lid of a round snuff box, on which the orbits of the planets are traced in diamonds. Made in the 1780s, it was the work of Johann Gottlieb Scharff, a German goldsmith who was in the employ of Catherine II in Saint Petersburg (Fig. 57). Another spectacular work is the underside of an oval box made in Vienna in the late eighteenth century. It boasts representations of the twelve months of the year – symbolised by precious stones – held by the sun's rays, which are set with diamonds (Fig. 58).

The lavish Baroque lifestyle enjoyed by noble families and the upper ranks of the clergy was also reflected in the treasures made by goldsmiths. More than ever, the sun, moon and stars were the motifs with which extravagant social aspirations could be demonstrated in an ostentatious context – probably also due to the growing interest in astronomy and cosmological issues.

19. JAHRHUNDERT

Kaum eine Epoche hat so viel „himmlischen" Schmuck hervorgebracht wie das 19. Jahrhundert. Magische, mythologische oder gar religiöse Motive waren – in der Folge von Aufklärung, Klassizismus und Empire – im Schmuck jener Zeit nur noch wenig relevant. Vorherrschend war nun das dekorative Element – auch bei der Darstellung der Gestirne. Schon gegen Ende des 18. Jahrhunderts verwendete man den Sternenhimmel im dekorativen Sinne, beispielsweise auf emaillierten Uhrgehäusen. Oft waren sie umrahmt von einem Perlenkranz und von zierlichen Blümchen, die sich als Symbole von Freundschaft und Liebe verstehen lassen (Abb. 60). Um 1800 findet sich in Frankreich ein ähnliches Motiv auch auf einem sogenannten Freundschaftsring: Die 25 goldenen Sterne auf blau emailliertem Grund sind umrahmt von einer Blüten- und Blattgirlande (Abb. 59). Sie weisen das Schmuckstück als ein Zeichen der Liebe und Verbundenheit aus.

Sonne, Mond und Sterne werden gesellschaftsfähig

Besonders in der zweiten Hälfte des 19. Jahrhunderts kam Schmuck mit Himmelskörpern in Mode. Die Gemahlin des Romanow-Großfürsten Vladimir, Marie zu Mecklenburg, trug beispielsweise anlässlich eines im Jahr 1875 ausgerichteten Kostümfests in Sankt Petersburg ein Diadem, das aus einer riesigen Diamantsonne mit einem zentralen Smaragd bestand.[53] Weitaus bekannter sind allerdings die Sterne des Wiener Juweliers Köchert, die Kaiserin Elisabeth („Sisi") von Österreich-Ungarn in ihrem Haar trug und die

59 Freundschaftsring, Frankreich, um 1800, Gold, Email. Friendship ring, France, c.1800, gold, enamel.
Schmuckmuseum Pforzheim, Inv. 1963-85

60 Daniel-François Vauchez, Damenuhr, Paris, um 1775, Gold, Email, Perlen. Daniel-François Vauchez, ladies' watch, Paris, c.1775, gold, enamel, pearls. Schmuckmuseum Pforzheim, Inv. 1974/10

THE NINETEENTH CENTURY

The nineteenth century brought forth more 'heavenly' jewellery than any other era. Magical, mythological and even devotional motifs were – following on the age of Enlightenment, neo-Classicism and the Empire style – not really relevant in the jewellery of the times. The predominant quality was now the decorative aspect, and this also held for the heavenly bodies as jewellery motifs. By the close of the eighteenth century, the starry firmament was used in the decorative sense – for instance, on enamelled watch cases. They were often framed by a wreath of pearls and graceful little flowers that can be interpreted as symbols of friendship and love (Fig. 60). In France c.1800 a similar motif occurs on what have always been known as friendship rings: one of these features twenty-five gold stars on a blue enamel ground framed by a garland of flowers and leaves (Fig. 59). They indicate that this piece of jewellery was a sign of love and attachment.

61 Franz Xaver Winterhalter, *Kaiserin Elisabeth von Österreich* (Detail), 1865, Öl auf Leinwand, 255 × 133 cm. Franz Xaver Winterhalter, *Empress Elisabeth of Austria* (detail), 1865, oil on canvas, 255 × 133 cm. Kunsthistorisches Museum Wien

The sun, moon and stars in high society

In the latter half of the nineteenth century especially, jewellery featuring the heavenly bodies became fashionable. In 1875 Marie of Mecklenburg, wife of Grand Duke Alexandrovich, a son of the Romanov emperor Alexander II, wore a diadem consisting of a huge diamond sun set with an emerald at its centre at a costume ball in Saint Petersburg.[53] The stars created by the Viennese jeweller Köchert, which Elisabeth ('Sisi'), Empress of Austria-Hungary, wore in her hair, are far better known and probably owe much of their worldwide renown to the 1865 portrait of her by Franz Xaver Winterhalter (Fig. 61). At that time star diadems and moon pins left goldsmiths' workshops and jewellers' shops not only in Vienna but also in London, Paris, Berlin, Saint Petersburg, New York and other great cities to represent the brilliance, magnificence and wealth of high society at lavishly and sumptuously staged festivities and balls.

Quite some time before Empress Sisi sparked off what amounted to a star jewellery cult, Virginia Oldoini, Countess Castiglione, was wearing decorative stars. However, unlike the Austrian empress, the beloved of both Napoleon III of France and Vittorio Emanuele of Italy was adorning not just her magnificent head of hair with them: diamond stars made by Maison Boucheron in Paris were scattered across her entire dress (Fig. 63). And yet society ladies tended to wear their most precious jewels in their hair. Their diadems and tiaras of gold or silver were usually richly set with diamonds, also in part with coloured precious stones and pearls. A remarkable piece in this connection is a diadem made in 1870 by Garrard of London. It was constructed in such a way that the nine diamond stars of the diadem could be removed and – as in the case of Empress Elisabeth – worn individually in the hair (Fig. 62). Sophia of Württemberg is also wearing five diamond stars in her hair in another Winterhalter portrait (Fig. 66). A design for a hairpin, which came from the Paris jeweller Alexis Falize, furnishes proof that stars set with precious stones could also be worn in other ways (Fig. 65).

Celebrities such as famous actresses and opera divas also wore star jewellery in their hair as well as star brooches and earrings. The motif was occasionally combined with a crescent moon pendant, as is documented by a portrait (c.1886) of Sophie Menter, pianist and music teacher (Fig. 64). Crescent moon brooches, often set with precious stones or pearls, were also widespread accessories worn on clothing (Fig. 67). An 1870s photograph of a young Frenchwomen named Mademoiselle Doinel shows the sitter wearing a brooch of that kind in her hair and combining it with a (presumably velvet) ribbon choker decorated with stars (Fig. 68). Another French photograph, dating from the 1880s, is a portrait of Gabrielle Boucheron, wife of the Paris jeweller Frédéric Boucheron. She, too, is wearing a lunula brooch in her hair (Fig. 69).

In the Islamic world, jewellery with moon and star motifs assumed particular significance: in 1889 Tancrède Dumas, an Italian photographer who was very famous in his day, took a photograph of a Turkish lady who is wearing both a crescent moon and a star brooch in her hair. These pieces of jewellery should probably be interpreted in this context as symbols of the Ottoman Empire, to which the wearer is patriotically paying homage (Fig. 70).

The combination of a lunula set with precious stones and a star in a single piece of jewellery has been recorded in England since about 1800 (Fig. 71). This is probably jewellery to be worn on a turban – a type that survived on into the

62 Garrard, Stern-Diadem, London, 1870, Gold, Silber, Diamanten, Privatsammlung. Garrard, Star tiara, London, 1870, gold, silver, diamonds, private collection

wohl auch dank des Porträts von Franz Xaver Winterhalter aus dem Jahr 1865 internationale Berühmtheit erlangten (Abb. 61). Nicht nur in Wien, auch in London, Paris, Berlin, Sankt Petersburg, New York und anderen Metropolen verließen damals Sterndiademe und Mondagraffen die Werkstätten der Goldschmiede und Juweliere, um dann auf üppig inszenierten Festen und Bällen Glanz, Pracht und Reichtum der feinen Gesellschaft vorzuführen.

Schon einige Zeit bevor Kaiserin Sisi geradezu einen Kult des Sternenschmucks ausgelöst hatte, trug Virginia Oldoini, die Gräfin von Castiglione, die schmückenden Sterne. Doch anders als die österreichische Kaiserin verzierte die Geliebte sowohl Napoleons III. als auch des italienischen Königs Vittorio Emmanuele damit nicht nur ihr prachtvolles Haar: Die im Hause Boucheron in Paris hergestellten Diamantsterne verteilten sich über das ganze Gewand (Abb. 63). Und doch war die Frisur der eigentliche Ort, an dem die Damen der vornehmen Gesellschaft ihre kostbaren Geschmeide trugen. Ihre Diademe und Tiaren aus Gold oder Silber

63 Virginia Oldoini, *Contessa Verasis di Castiglione (1837–1899)*, um 1865, Fotografie. Virginia Oldoini, *Countess Verasis di Castiglione (1837–1899)*, c.1865, photograph

64 Bildnis der der Sophie Menter mit Lunula-Anhänger und sternförmigen Ohrringen, um 1886. Portrait of Sophie Menter with lunula pendant and star-shaped earrings, c.1886

waren meist reich mit Diamanten, teilweise aber auch mit farbigen Edelsteinen und Perlen besetzt. Bemerkenswert ist in diesem Zusammenhang ein im Londoner Hause Garrard hergestelltes Diadem aus dem Jahr 1870. Es wurde so konstruiert, dass die neun Diamantsterne abgenommen werden und – wie im Falle von Kaiserin Elisabeth – einzeln im Haar getragen werden konnten (Abb. 62). Auch Sophia von Württemberg trägt auf einem von Winterhalter geschaffenen Porträt fünf Diamantsterne im Haar (Abb. 66). Einen Hinweis darauf, dass edelsteinbesetzte Sterne aber auch in anderer Weise getragen werden konnten, gibt ein Entwurf für einen Haarstecker, der von dem Pariser Juwelier Alexis Falize stammt (Abb. 65).

Berühmte Persönlichkeiten wie gefeierte Schauspielerinnen und Operndiven trugen nun ebenfalls Sternenschmuck im Haar sowie Sternbroschen und -ohrringe.

65 Alexis Falize, Entwurf für einen Stern-Haarstecker, Paris, 2. Hälfte 19. Jh. Alexis Falize, sketch for a hairpin with stars, Paris, latter half of the 19th century

66 Franz Xaver Winterhalter, *Prinzessin Sophia Frederika Mathilda von Württemberg*, 1863–1873, Öl auf Leinwand, 74 × 60 cm. Franz Xaver Winterhalter, *Princess Sophia Frederika Mathilda of Württemberg*, 1863–1873, oil on canvas, 74 × 60 cm. Rijksmuseum, Amsterdam, Inv. SK-A-1702

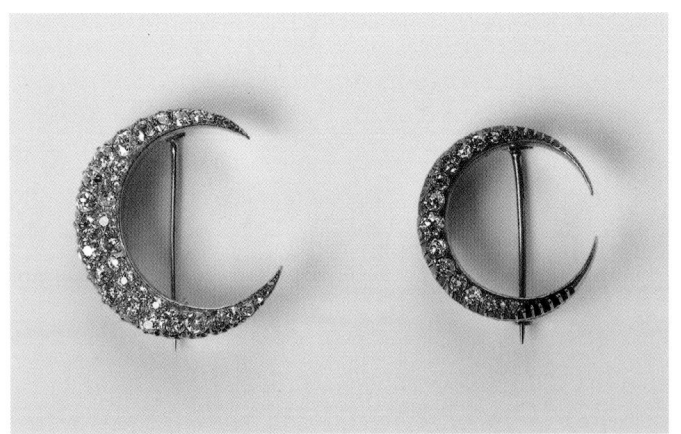 

67 Mondsichel-Broschen, 19. und 20. Jh., Silber, Gold, Diamanten, Privatsammlung. Crescent-moon brooches, 19th and 20th century, silver, gold, diamonds, private collection

68 Bildnis der Mademoiselle Doinel mit sternenbesetztem Halsband, um 1870. Portrait of Mademoiselle Doinel wearing a choker with diamond-set stars, c.1870

Gelegentlich wurde das Motiv mit einem Mondsichelanhänger kombiniert, wie dies ein Bildnis der Pianistin und Musikpädagogin Sophie Menter aus der Zeit um 1886 dokumentiert (Abb. 64). Verbreitet waren auch Mondsichelbroschen die, häufig mit Edelsteinen oder Perlen besetzt, an der Kleidung getragen wurden (Abb. 67). Auf der Fotografie einer jungen Französin namens Mademoiselle Doinel aus den Siebzigerjahren des 19. Jahrhunderts trägt die Dargestellte eine solche Brosche im Haar und kombiniert sie mit einem mit Sternen verzierten Halsband (vermutlich aus Samt; Abb. 68). Eine weitere Fotografie aus den 1880ern zeigt Gabrielle Boucheron, die Ehefrau des Pariser Juweliers Frédéric Boucheron. Auch sie trägt eine Lunula-Brosche im Haar (Abb. 69).

In der muslimischen Welt nahm der Schmuck mit Mond- und Sternmotiven eine besondere Bedeutung an: So lichtete der zu seiner Zeit hochberühmte italienische Fotograf Tancrède Dumas 1889 eine türkische Dame ab, die sowohl eine Mondsichel als auch eine Sternbrosche im Haar trägt. Diese Schmuckstücke dürfen in diesem Kontext wohl als Symbole des osmanischen Reiches gedeutet werden, dem die Trägerin patriotisch huldigt (Abb. 70).

Die Kombination einer edelsteinbesetzten Lunula und eines Sterns in einem einzigen Schmuckstück ist in England seit der Zeit um 1800 belegt (Abb. 71). Vermutlich handelt es sich dabei um Turbanschmuck – ein Typus, der sich als Zier orientalischer Kopfbedeckungen bis ins 20. Jahrhundert erhalten hat. Ein im Jahre 1957 von Garrard in London für einen malayischen Fürsten geschaffenes Stück mag hierfür als Beispiel gelten.[54]

69 Gabrielle Boucheron, gekleidet für einen Kostümball, 1880/90, Fotografie. Gabrielle Boucheron, dressed for a costume ball, 1880/90, photograph. Collection Radius et Margelidon

70 Tancrède R. Dumas, *Türkische Dame in Damaskus*, 1889, Fotografie.
Tancrède R. Dumas, *Turkish Woman in Damascus*, 1889, photograph.
Library of Congress, Prints and Photographs Division, Washington D.C.

71 Haar- oder Turbanornament in Form einer Mondsichel mit einem Stern, England, um 1800, Gold, Perlen, rosa Topaze, B 5,4 cm. Hair or turban ornament in the shape of a crescent moon with a star, England, c.1800, gold, pearls and pink topazes. British Museum, London, Inv. 1978,1002.208

twentieth century as decoration for oriental headgear. A piece made by Garrard of London in 1957 for a Malay prince is worth citing in this connection.[54]

Brooches created by Tiffany in New York in 1876 to commemorate the centenary of the Declaration of Independence show that the star motif could be used to make a patriotic statement in the West as well. The first thirteen states that constituted the young United States of America are represented on the brooch *The Star-Spangled Banner (Stars and Stripes)* by one diamond each. This piece of jewellery not only commemorated the great event but served to showcase the wearer's patriotic awareness.[55]

72 Alphonse Fouquet, Diadem, 1883, H 11,5 cm, B 16 cm. Alphonse Fouquet, tiara, 1883, H 11.5, W 16 cm

73 Julienne, Parure *Milchstraße*, Paris, um 1860/65. Julienne, *Milky Way* parure, Paris, c.1860/65. Robin archives

74 René Lalique, Aigrette *Galaxie*, Paris, 1890/1898, Silber, Gold, Diamanten, Federn, Privatsammlung. René Lalique, *Galaxie* aigrette, Paris, 1890/1898, silver, gold, diamonds, feathers, private collection

Dass das Sternenmotiv auch im Westen eine patriotische Aussage haben konnte, zeigen Broschen, die von Tiffany 1876 in New York anlässlich der hundertsten Wiederkehr der Unabhängigkeitserklärung kreiert wurden. In der Brosche *The Star-Spangled Banner (Stars and Stripes)* werden die Sterne für die ersten 13 freien Staaten von Nordamerika durch je einen Diamanten repräsentiert. Das Schmuckstück diente neben der Erinnerung an das große Ereignis zur öffentlichen Darstellung patriotischen Bewusstseins.[55]

Extravagant, reizvoll und sehr ungewöhnlich ist ein Diadem, das der Pariser Juwelier Alphonse Fouquet im Jahre 1883 schuf: Die goldene geflügelte Büste einer jungen Frau ist bekrönt von einem Stern, der mit einem großen Diamanten ausgefasst wurde (Abb. 72).

Generell kann festgestellt werden, dass wohl alle bedeutenden Juweliere – sowohl in der französischen Hauptstadt als auch weit darüber hinaus – den Kosmos als Motiv in ihre Kreationen einbezogen: die Goldschmiededynastien der Robin (Abb. 73), der Falize, der Boucheron und der Fouquet ebenso wie der junge René Lalique. Vermutlich zwischen 1890 und 1898 – noch bevor er zum überragenden Meister des Art-Nouveau-Schmuckes geworden war – schuf er ganz im Sinne der Belle Époque eine Aigrette mit Sternen und Federn (Abb. 74).

75 Benckiser & Co., Medaillon-Anhänger, Pforzheim, 1869, Gold, Türkise, Perlen. Benckiser & Co., medallion pendant, Pforzheim, 1869, gold, turquoise, pearls. Schmuckmuseum Pforzheim, Inv. KV 784

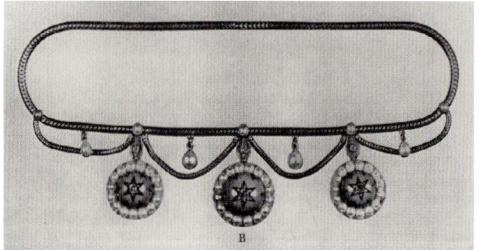

76 Parkes of Vigo Street, Kollier, London, um 1868, Goldkette mit drei Medaillon-Anhängern in hellblauem Email, besetzt mit einem Diamantstern und gerahmt von Perlen. Parkes of Vigo Street, necklet, London, c.1868, gold chain with three pendant medallions, each in light-blue enamel set with a diamond star and surrounded with pearls

77   *Sortie de bal* (Detail), aus dem *Journal des Demoiselles*, März 1854. *Sortie de bal* (detail), from *Journal des Demoiselles*, March 1854

An extravagant, attractive and very unusual creation is a diadem made in 1883 by the Paris jeweller Alphonse Fouquet: a gold winged bust of a young woman is crowned by a star filled out with a large diamond (Fig. 72).

On the whole, it can be noted that probably all important jewellers – both in the French capital and far beyond it – incorporated the cosmos as a motif in their creations: the French goldsmith dynasties such as the Robins (Fig. 73), the Falizes, the Boucherons and the Fouquets as well as the young René Lalique all did so. Presumably between 1890 and 1898 – even before he became the supreme master of Art Nouveau jewellery – Lalique had created an aigrette with stars and feathers entirely in the belle époque spirit (Fig. 74).

Alongside the jewellers, the jewellery industry was developing rapidly and also producing remarkable pieces. Hence cosmic motifs found a niche not only in the jewellery worn by the nobility, aristocracy and the emergent affluent bourgeoisie but also that favoured by the rural classes who tended to live in modest circumstances. Pendant medallions with star motifs were evidently highly popular everywhere. Extremely costly pieces of this kind were made at Chaumet in Paris, for instance, while the flourishing workshops and jewellery factories in London, Birmingham and Pforzheim were turning out simpler pieces – often silver-gilt or silver-plated (Figs. 75-78). Moreover, the Bohemian garnet-jewellery industry devoted a great deal of attention to the heavenly bodies in brooches, pendants and ear jewellery (Fig. 79).

78   Adie & Lovekin, Brosche, Birmingham, um 1880, Gold, Silber. Adie & Lovekin, brooch, Birmingham, c.1880, gold, silver. Schmuckmuseum Pforzheim, Inv. KV 105

Neben den Juwelieren brachte nun aber auch die sich rasant entwickelnde Schmuckindustrie bemerkenswerte Stücke hervor. Die kosmischen Motive fanden ihren Platz daher nicht nur im Schmuck des Adels und des aufstrebenden, wohlhabend gewordenen Bürgertums, sondern auch bei Bevölkerungsschichten im ländlichen Raum, die eher in bescheidenen Verhältnissen lebten. Medaillonanhänger mit Sternmotiven erfreuten sich offenbar überall besonderer Beliebtheit. So entstanden beispielsweise bei Chaumet in Paris äußerst kostbare Exemplare, während die aufblühenden Werkstätten und Fabriken in London, Birmingham und Pforzheim einfachere Stücke – häufig aus vergoldetem Silber – produzierten (Abb. 75-78). Darüber hinaus widmete die böhmische Granatschmuckindustrie den Gestirnen in Broschen, Anhängern und Ohrschmuck große Aufmerksamkeit (Abb. 79).

Rückbezug auf historische Vorbilder
Der in der zweiten Hälfte des 19. Jahrhunderts die Künste dominierende Historismus war nicht nur in Malerei, Architektur und Bildhauerkunst prägend, sondern wirkte sich auch auf die Gestaltung von Schmuck aus. Große Goldschmiedepersönlichkeiten wie beispielsweise Augusto Pio Castellani in Rom befassten sich intensiv mit antikem Schmuck und den alten Goldschmiedetechniken. So glaubte Castel-

79 Halskette, Böhmen (?), 2. Hälfte 19. Jh., Granate, Schenkung von ISSP. Necklace, Bohemia (?), latter half of the 19th century, garnets, donation by ISSP. Schmuckmuseum Pforzheim, Inv. 2008/55

80 Castellani, „Helios"-Brosche, Italien, um 1860–1880, Gold, gegossen, Augen eingelegt in Email, Goldgranulation. Castellani, 'Helios' brooch, Italy, c.1860–1880, gold, cast, enamelled eyes, gold granulation. British Museum, London, Inv. 1978,1002.734

81 Streeter & Co., Brosche mit einer Darstellung des ägyptischen Skarabäus Khepri, der Personifikation des Ra, London, um 1868–1875, Gold, Golddraht, Dm 4,4 cm. Streeter & Co., brooch featuring the Egyptian scarab beetle Khepri, the personification of Ra, London, c.1868–1875, gold, gold wire, dia. 4.4 cm. British Museum, London, Inv. 1978,1002.44

lani, die echte etruskische Granulation wiederentdeckt zu haben, was ihm letztlich aber doch nicht gelungen war. Eine hellenistische Brosche mit dem Bild des Helios (s. Abb. 36) aus seiner Sammlung antiken Schmucks diente Castellani als Vorbild für eine seiner historisierenden Broschen. Als Kreation des 19. Jahrhunderts stellt sie seine Bewunderung für die mythologisch geprägte Schmuckgestaltung der Antike unter Beweis (Abb. 80). Eine verwandte künstlerische Haltung äußert sich in einer etwa zeitgleich entstandenen historisierenden Brosche aus England: Sie zeigt einen Skarabäus, den heiligen Käfer der Ägypter, mit der Sonnenscheibe (Abb. 81).[56]

Ein Motiv, das in der zweiten Hälfte des 19. Jahrhunderts wohl ohne magischen oder gar religiösen Hintergrund entwickelt wurde, ist der sogenannte „Sunburst". Die Strahlen dieser abstrahierten aufgehenden Sonne, die oft als Brosche oder Mittelpunkt von Diademen diente, waren meist mit Diamanten besetzt. Ein

82 Carl Fabergé, Kassette mit Starburst-Applikationen, um 1900, Nephrit, Gold, Diamanten, Rubine, B 7 cm, T 3 cm. Carl Fabergé, stamp box with starburst applications, c.1900, nephrite, gold, diamonds, rubies, W 7 cm, D 3 cm. Wartski, London

The return to historical models

Historicism, which was the dominant period style in the latter half of the nineteenth century, not only shaped painting, architecture and sculpture but also had an impact on jewellery design. Distinguished goldsmiths, such as Augusto Pio Castellani in Rome, dedicated themselves to intensive study of ancient jewellery and old goldsmithing techniques. Castellani believed he had rediscovered the genuine Etruscan granulation process but ultimately proved unsuccessful because he was mistaken. A Hellenistic brooch with an image of Helios (see Fig. 36) from Castellani's collection of ancient jewellery was the model for one of his historicising brooches. As a nineteenth-century creation, the brooch testifies to its creator's admiration of the mythology-based jewellery design of Greco-Roman antiquity (Fig. 80). A similar artistic stance is expressed in a historicising brooch from England of roughly the same date: it features a scarab, the sacred beetle of ancient Egypt, with the sun disc (Fig. 81).[56]

A motif that was developed in the latter half of the nineteenth century, probably without any magical or even religious overtones, is the type known as a

83 Sunburst-Diadem, Frankreich, um 1900, Platin, Diamanten.
Sunburst tiara, France, c.1900, platinum, diamonds. Wartski, London

besonders schönes Beispiel hierfür ist eine Aigrette von Joseph Chaumet, die allerdings erst um 1914 entstanden ist (Abb. 84) Gelegentlich fand das Motiv auch auf kleineren Gegenständen des täglichen Gebrauchs Verwendung, wie etwa eine Fabergé-Dose aus Nephrit beweist (Abb. 82).

Eines der spektakulärsten Sunburst-Schmuckstücke ist eine in England geschaffene Brosche aus der Zeit um 1890, die sich vorübergehend im Besitz von Jacqueline Kennedy Onassis befand.[57] Das Motiv hat sich bis ins 20. Jahrhundert hinein erhalten: Noch um 1900 entstand – vermutlich in Paris – eine zarte Tiara (Abb. 83), 1921 wurde ein sehr aufwändiges Diadem bei Cartier in Paris geschaffen,[58] und noch 1973 setzte sich der Londoner Schmuckkünstler Andrew Grima in einer Brosche mit dem Sunburst-Thema auseinander.[59]

84 Joseph Chaumet, Aigrette *Lever du Soleil* (Sonnenaufgang), 1914, Platin, Smaragd, Diamanten, Federn, H 5,5 cm, B 13 cm. Joseph Chaumet, *Lever du Soleil* (Rising Sun) aigrette, 1914, platinum, emerald, diamonds, feathers, H 5.5 cm, W 13 cm. Collection Chaumet, Paris

85 Victor Mayer, Fabergé-Werkmeister, *Mondphasenuhr-Ei*, Pforzheim, 2000, Gold, Email, Diamanten, Saphire, Bergkristall, Onyx, Rosenquarz. Victor Mayer, workmaster of Fabergé, *Egg with Phases of the Moon Clock*, Pforzheim, 2000, gold, enamel, diamonds, sapphires, rock crystal, onyx, rose quartz, onyx. Courtesy of Draguljarna Malalan, Ljubljana

'sunburst'. The rays of this abstract rising sun, which often served as a brooch or the centrepiece of a diadem, were usually set with diamonds. A particularly handsome example is an aigrette by Joseph Chaumet, which, however, was not made until about 1914 (Fig. 84). The sunburst motif occasionally occurs on smaller objects that were in daily use, such as a Fabergé box made of nephrite (Fig. 82).

One of the most spectacular sunburst jewels is a brooch made in England c.1890, which was once owned by Jacqueline Kennedy Onassis.[57] The motif survived on into the twentieth century: a delicate tiara (Fig. 83) dates to c.1900, presumably from Paris; a very elaborate diadem was made by Cartier in Paris in 1921;[58] and as late as 1973 the London art jewellery maker Andrew Grima was still investigating the sunburst theme, this time as a brooch.[59]

Fabergé and the heavenly bodies

The metropolis on the Neva, Saint Petersburg, became, as the capital of the vast Russian Empire, a centre of art and jewellery making. The goldsmith, jeweller and successful entrepreneur Peter Carl Fabergé worked there. His fame, which endures untarnished to this day, was based on the unique Easter eggs in gold, silver, precious stones, pearls and the most exquisite enamel he and his workmasters created on commission for the imperial family from 1885 on.

Fabergé also devoted himself in precious decorative appointments – luxury articles and other items for daily use – to the heavenly bodies. An Easter egg from 1917, presumably one of the last to have been designed by Carl Fabergé personally, also featured a cosmic motif: conceived as a world clock, it was fitted out with a celestial globe.[60] However, political events prevented the work, which was intended as a present for Tsarina Alexandra, being finished. The Victor Mayer manufactory, which was successful in Pforzheim in the late twentieth and early twenty-first centuries as a Fabergé workmaster, took up the idea in 2004 and created a moon-phase clock which is entirely in the tradition of the Petersburg master (Fig. 85).

Exquisite table clocks and alarm clocks with allusions to the heavenly bodies were made at the Fabergé workshops c.1900, often after designs by Henrik Wigström and Mikhail Perkhin (Fig. 87).[61] Largely unaffected by Art Nouveau and Jugendstil, these clocks are stylistically still rooted in the nineteenth century.

In addition, an entire series of gold cigarette cases from Maison Fabergé boasts the crescent moon motif (Figs. 88-90). They were made between 1901 and 1915 as presents for the French spy and adventurer Charles Antoine Roger Luzarche d'Azay.[62] One of these cigarette cases bears the motto of the Prince of Wales ('ICH DIEN'; German: 'I serve') and a silver crescent moon open to the left. On another, a frontally represented elephant has a crescent moon on its forehead. And a lunula set with diamonds adorns the third case.

In 1913, after Art Nouveau had long since gone out of fashion in France, Fabergé produced a design drawing of a pendant that is clearly a lingering echo of that movement: a swallow strongly reminiscent of René Lalique's elegant birds is flying above a sea from which the sun is rising (Fig. 86) – a late tribute to Art Nouveau and Jugendstil.

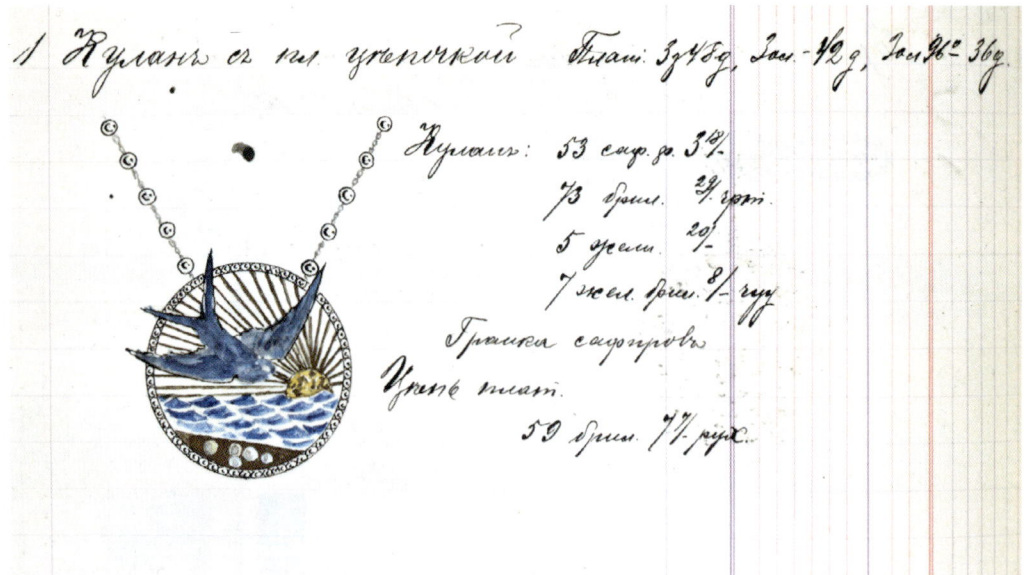

86 Carl Fabergé, Entwurfszeichnung für einen Anhänger, 1913.
Carl Fabergé, sketch for a pendant, 1913. Courtesy of Wartski, London

Fabergé und die Gestirne

Die Metropole an der Newa, Sankt Petersburg, war als Hauptstadt des riesigen Zarenreiches zu einem Zentrum von Kunst und Kultur geworden. Dort war der Goldschmied, Juwelier und erfolgreiche Geschäftsmann Peter Carl Fabergé tätig. Sein bis zum heutigen Tage andauernder Ruhm wurde durch die einzigartigen Ostereier aus Gold, Silber, Edelsteinen, Perlen und feinstem Email begründet, die er und seine Werkmeister im Auftrag der Zarenfamilie seit 1885 kreierten.

Auch Fabergé befasste sich in kostbaren Gerätschaften – Luxusgegenstände und solche, die zum täglichen Gebrauch dienten – mit den Gestirnen. Ein im Jahre 1917 vermutlich von Carl Fabergé selbst entworfenes letztes Osterei wies ebenfalls ein kosmisches Motiv auf: Es war als Weltenuhr konzipiert und mit einem Himmelsglobus ausgestattet.[60] Doch aufgrund der politischen Ereignisse konnte das Geschenk für die Zarin Alexandra nicht mehr fertiggestellt werden. Die Manufaktur Victor Mayer, die Ende des 20. und Anfang des 21. Jahrhunderts als Fabergé-Werkmeister erfolgreich in Pforzheim wirkte, nahm die Idee auf und schuf im Jahre 2004 ein Mondphasenuhr-Ei, das ganz in der Tradition des Petersburger Meisters steht (Abb. 85).

87 Maison Fabergé, Werkmeister Henrik Wigström, Tischuhr *Der Mann im Mond*, St. Petersburg, 1908–1917, Gold, Silber, Diamanten in Rosenschliff, Perlen, Bergkristall, guillochiert, Email. House of Fabergé, workmaster Henrik Wigström, desk timepiece *The Man in the Moon*, St Petersburg, 1908–1917, gold, silver, rose-cut diamonds, pearls, rock crystal, foil, carving, rolling, guilloche enamel, champlevé enamel, matting. Fabergé Museum, St. Petersburg, The Link of Times Foundation

88 Maison Carl Fabergé, Werkmeister Henrik Wigström, Zigarettenetui mit Elefant und Mondsichel, St. Petersburg, um 1910, Gold, Platin, Diamanten, Email, Zunder, 10 × 6,2 cm. House of Carl Fabergé, workmaster Henrik Wigström, cigarette case with elephant and crescent moon, St Petersburg, c.1910, gold, platinum, diamonds, enamel, tinder cord, 10 × 6.2 cm. Les Arts décoratifs – Musée des Arts décoratifs, Paris, Département Art Nouveau / Art Déco, Inv. 38343

89 Maison Carl Fabergé, Werkmeister Henrik Wigström und Alphonse Eugène Lechevrel, Zigarettenetui in Samorodok-Technik, St. Petersburg, um 1906, Gold, Diamant, Saphir, Silber, Baumwolle, 9,8 × 6,4 cm. House of Carl Fabergé, workmaster Henrik Wigström and Alphonse Eugène Lechevrel, cigarette case, Samorodok technique, St Petersburg, c.1906, gold, diamond, sapphire, silver, cotton, 9.8 × 6.4 cm. Les Arts décoratifs – Musée des Arts décoratifs, Paris, Département Art Nouveau / Art Déco, Paris, Inv. 39449

Um 1900 entstanden in Fabergés Werkstätten, oft nach Entwürfen von Henrik Wigström und Michail Perchin, zudem kostbare Uhren, die sich als Tischuhren und Wecker auf die Gestirne bezogen (Abb. 87).[61] Weitgehend unberührt von Art Nouveau und Jugendstil, sind sie stilistisch noch dem 19. Jahrhundert zuzurechnen.

Mit dem Motiv der Mondsichel ausgestattet ist außerdem eine ganze Serie goldener Zigarettendosen aus dem Hause Fabergé (Abb. 88–90). Sie wurden zwischen 1901 und 1915 als Geschenke für den französischen Geheimagenten und Abenteurer Charles Antoine Roger Luzarche d'Azay geschaffen.[62] Eines dieser Etuis ist mit dem Motto des Prince of Wales („ICH DIEN") und mit einer nach links offenen silbernen Mondsichel versehen. Auf einem anderen trägt ein frontal dargestellter Elefant eine Mondsichel auf der Stirn. Und auf einem dritten befindet sich eine diamantbesetzte Lunula.

Im Jahre 1913, als in Frankreich der Art Nouveau längst aus der Mode gekommen war, entstand im Hause Fabergé eine Entwurfszeichnung für einen Anhänger, der ganz in der Nachfolge dieser Bewegung steht: Eine Schwalbe, die sehr an die eleganten Vögel des René Lalique erinnert, fliegt über das Meer, über dem gerade die Sonne aufgeht (Abb. 86) – eine späte Erinnerung an Art Nouveau und Jugendstil.

Sonne und Mond im volkstümlichen Schmuck

In der Region um Neapel – und wohl nur dort – ist seit dem frühen 19. Jahrhundert ein silbernes Amulett verbreitet, das sich großer Beliebtheit erfreute und sich bis zum heutigen Tage erhalten hat: der sogenannte Cimaruta-Anhänger.[63] In verschiedenen Zusammenstellungen finden sich hier unheilabwehrende beziehungsweise Glück bringende Zeichen: Herzen haltende Händchen, kleine Vögel, Schlüssel und – ganz wichtig – Abbilder der Sonne und des Mondes. Trotz aller moderner Aufgeklärtheit werden hier offensichtlich die magischen Kräfte der Himmelskörper für den die Cimaruta tragenden Menschen auf den Plan gerufen.

„Himmlisch" waren viele Schmuckstücke und Preziosen während des ganzen 19. Jahrhunderts. Die Gestirne prägten die Goldschmiede- und Schmuckkunst dieser Epoche zwar nicht ausschließlich, doch waren sie wichtige Bestandteile der Gestaltung in einer Zeit, die sonst so viele unterschiedliche Kunstformen und Stile hervorgebracht hat.

90   Maison Carl Fabergé, Werkmeister Henrik Wigström, Zigarettenetui, St. Petersburg, um 1909, Gold, Silber, Email, Platin, Diamant, 10,2 × 6,7 cm.
House of Carl Fabergé, workmaster Henrik Wigström, cigarette case, St Petersburg, c.1909, gold, silver, enamel, platinum, diamond, 10.2 × 6.7 cm.
Les Arts décoratifs – Musée des Arts décoratifs, Paris, Département Art Nouveau / Art Déco, Paris, Inv. 39454

Sun and moon in folkloric jewellery

In the Naples region — and probably only there — a type of silver amulet has been widespread since the early nineteenth century. Once very popular indeed, it has survived to the present day: what is known as a *cimaruta* [Italian: 'sprig of rue'] pendant.[63] In variously combined compositions it unites apotropaic and good luck signs: hands holding hearts, little birds, keys and — very importantly — representations of the sun and moon. Defying the enlightenment of the modern age, the magical powers of the heavenly bodies are evidently still very much on the cards for people wearing the *cimaruta*.

Many pieces of jewellery and precious objects made throughout the nineteenth century were 'heavenly' in both senses of the word. The heavenly bodies were not, however, the only motifs to figure prominently in goldsmiths' work and jewellery of the time although they were important elements of design in an era that saw the emergence of so many different art forms and styles.

ART NOUVEAU

Der in der zweiten Hälfte des 19. Jahrhunderts in Kunst, Architektur und Kunsthandwerk vorherrschende Historismus verliert ab ungefähr 1895 stark an Bedeutung. Eine „neue Kunst" bricht sich Bahn – in Frankreich als Art Nouveau, in England in der Arts-and-Crafts-Bewegung, in Österreich unter dem Überbegriff Sezession und in Deutschland als Jugendstil. Der deutsche Name nimmt dabei Bezug auf die Münchner Kunst- und Kulturzeitschrift *Jugend*. Statt sich historischer Vorbilder und Motive zu bedienen, verwandelten die neuen Bewegungen oft das Bild der Natur – seien es Pflanzen, Tiere oder der Mensch – in ornamentale Formen.

Vielfältig waren die Voraussetzungen, die diese revolutionären Entwicklungen beeinflussten und prägten. Nicht zuletzt war es die Kunst Japans, die in Europa und Amerika ab 1860 höchste Aufmerksamkeit und Bewunderung erfuhr, hatte sich das Land der aufgehenden Sonne nach jahrhundertelanger selbstgewählter Isolation doch nun dem Westen geöffnet. In der Glaskunst und im Möbelentwurf machten sich die Einflüsse aus Japan vorrangig in Nancy bemerkbar. Im Schmuck waren es die großen Pariser Meister, die sich nun auch von den traditionellen Gegenständen des täglichen Gebrauchs anregen ließen: etwa von den Inrō, modischen Gürtelaccessoires des japanischen Mannes (Abb. 92), oder von den kostbaren Zierkämmen der Frauen (Abb. 91), die für die Ausstattung ihrer kunstvollen Frisuren unerlässlich waren. Wie in Japan entwickelten sich auch in Europa und Amerika die Gestirne zu beliebten Gestaltungsmotiven, wobei der auf- und untergehenden Sonne besondere Aufmerksamkeit gewidmet wurde.

91 Zierkamm mit Vogel und Sonne, Japan, 19. Jh., Silber, Gold, Lack, 10,2 × 3,7 cm.
Decorative comb with bird and sun, 19th century, silver, gold, lacquer, 10,2 × 3,7 cm.
Les Arts décoratifs – Musée des Arts décoratifs, Paris, Département Art Nouveau / Art Déco, Paris, Inv. 7813

92 Inrō mit Regenpfeifern über Wellen bei Sonnenuntergang, 19. Jh., schwarzer Lackgrund mit Einlagen, verschiedene Lacktechniken, Ojime aus Koralle, 7,6 × 7,8 × 1,9 cm.
Inrō with design of ringed plovers over waves at sunset, 19th century, black lacquer ground with inlays, various lacquer techniques, coral ojime, 7.6 × 7.8 × 1.9 cm. Linden-Museum Stuttgart, Inv. OA 18.562 (TI 337)

93 René Lalique, Zierkamm mit Landschaft und untergehender Sonne, um 1900, Gold, Horn, Email. René Lalique, decorative comb with landscape and setting sun, *c*.1900, gold, horn, enamel. Musée Lalique, Wingen-sur-Moder, courtesy of Shai Bandmann & Ronald Ooi

ART NOUVEAU

From about 1895

Historicism, which had been the predominant movement in art, architecture and the decorative arts during the latter half of the nineteenth century, noticeably began to lose its pre-eminence. A 'new art' was forging ahead – in France as Art Nouveau, in the British Isles as the Arts and Crafts movement, in Austria under the heading 'Secession' and in Germany as Jugendstil. The German name for the movement refers to the Munich art and culture journal *Jugend*. Instead of using historical models and motifs, the new movements often represented transformations of nature's image – be the motifs flora, fauna or human – into ornamental forms.

The conditions that influenced and shaped these revolutionary developments were manifold. Not the least of these was Japanese art, which from 1860 attracted the most attention and admiration in Europe and America. After centuries of voluntary isolation, the Land of the Rising Sun had now opened itself to the West. In art glass and furniture design, the Japanese influences were primarily to be seen in Nancy. In jewellery it was the great Paris master jewellery makers and designers who now sought inspiration from traditional objects used in everyday life: for instance, from *inrō*, the fashionable sash accessories for Japanese gentlemen (Fig. 92), or from the exquisite ornamental hair combs worn by Japanese ladies (Fig. 91) as must-have additions to their sophisticated hairdos. As in Japan, the heavenly bodies also became popular design motifs in Europe and America, with particular attention devoted to the rising and the setting sun.

The sun motif

René Lalique, the most important master of Art Nouveau jewellery, created an elegant ornamental comb on which the *soleil couchant* – the setting sun – is reflected in a landscape of lakes at dusk (Fig. 93). A similar motif occurs in an enamel picture on a small pendant watch made in Switzerland *c*.1900. On it a gold wading bird is depicted standing at the edge of a body of water. It has just caught a snake while the setting sun forms an atmospheric backdrop (Fig. 95). French Art Nouveau belt buckles, on the other hand, often feature the symbolism of the rising sun: a young woman, for instance, framed by floral decoration, rejoices in a flower and the rays of the day star rising above the sea (Fig. 94).

The Paris artisan jeweller Léopold Gautrait also links the sun with nature – although in a far more sophisticated way: in a pendant that, thanks to his imaginative decorative design, is regarded as a masterpiece of Art Nouveau jewellery, the sunflower motif and the sun are indissolubly interwoven, a device that alludes to the life-giving powers of the sun in aesthetically cogent symbolism (Fig. 96). Gautrait also used the sunflower motif in a second pendant. In this case, he combined it with the delicate head of a young lady viewed in profile, her face turned to the left. Here, too, the statement the artist is making might be phrased as follows: the sun invigorates mankind and all of nature with its light and warmth and it is the revitalising powers of the sun that make life on earth possible in the first place (Fig. 97).

A poster (*c*.1900) launched by the Paris jewellers Crespin & Dufayel shows that the symbolic powers of the sun could be effectively deployed as a strategy

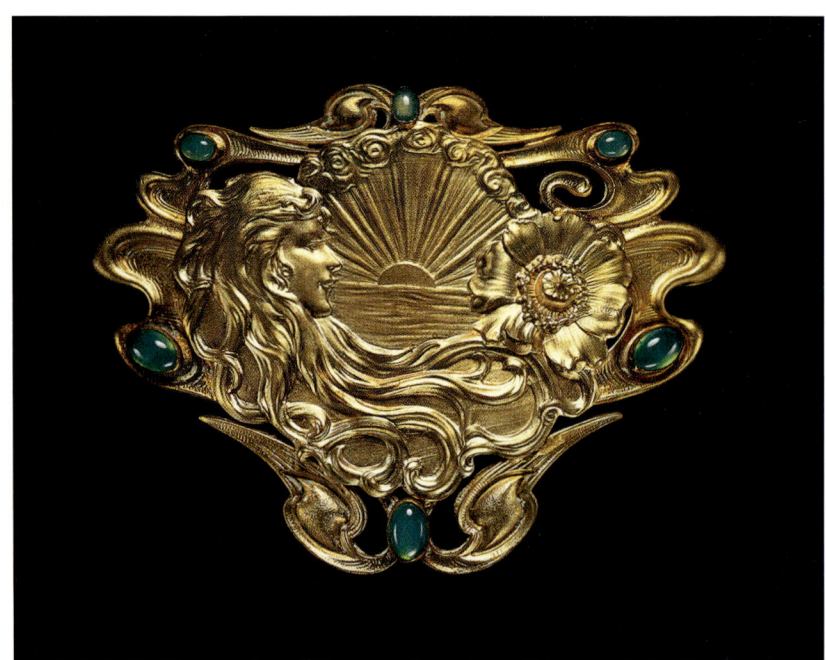

94 Gürtelschließe, Frankreich, um 1900, Metall, vergoldet, grüne Glassteine, 7 × 10 cm, ehem. Sammlung Kreuzer. Belt buckle, France, c.1900, metal-gilt, green glass stones, 7 × 10 cm, formerly Kreuzer Collection

Das Sonnenmotiv

René Lalique, der bedeutendste Meister der Art-Nouveau-Schmuckkunst, schuf einen eleganten Schmuckkamm, auf dem der *Soleil Couchant* – die untergehende Sonne – sich in einer abendlichen Seenlandschaft spiegelt (Abb. 93). Ein verwandtes Motiv findet sich auch auf dem Emailbild einer kleinen Anhängeuhr, die um 1900 in der Schweiz entstanden ist. Man sieht darauf einen goldenen Stelzvogel am Rande eines Gewässers stehen. Er hat gerade eine Schlange gefangen, während im Hintergrund stimmungsvoll die Abendsonne untergeht (Abb. 95). Französische Gürtelschließen des Art Nouveau hingegen beschäftigen sich häufig symbolhaft mit der aufgehenden Sonne: Eine junge Frau beispielsweise, umrahmt von floralen Ornamenten, erfreut sich einer Blüte und den Strahlen des über dem Meer aufsteigenden Tagesgestirns (Abb. 94).

Auch der Pariser Schmuckkünstler Léopold Gautrait verbindet die Sonne mit der Natur – allerdings auf weitaus raffiniertere Weise: In einem Anhänger, der dank seiner phantasievoll-ornamentalen Gestaltung als ein Meisterwerk der Art-Nouveau-Schmuckkunst gilt, sind das Motiv der Sonnenblume und der Sonne untrennbar miteinander verwoben, wodurch die Leben spendende Kraft ästhetisch greifbar wird (Abb. 96). Gautrait nutzte das Sonnenblumenmotiv auch in einem weiteren Anhänger. In diesem Falle kombinierte er es mit einem zierlichen Frauenköpfchen, das im Profil nach links gerichtet ist. Auch hier könnte die Aus-

95 Damen-Anhängeuhr, Schweiz, um 1900, Gold, Email. Ladies' pocket watch, Switzerland, *c.*1900, gold, enamel. Schmuckmuseum Pforzheim, Inv. KV 1357

96 Léopold Gautrait, Anhänger *Helianthus*, um 1900, Gold, Fensteremail, Perle, Diamant, Edelsteine, 11,4 × 4,7 cm. Léopold Gautrait, *Helianthus* pendant, *c.*1900, gold, plique à jour enamelling, pearl, diamond, precious stones, 11.4 × 4.7 cm. Courtesy of Tadema Gallery, London

97 Léopold Gautrait, Anhänger *Sonnenblume*, um 1900, Gold, Elfenbein, Fensteremail, Diamanten, Perle. Léopold Gautrait, *Sunflower* pendant, *c.*1900, gold, ivory, plique à jour enamelling, diamonds, pearl. Collection A. Aardewerk Antiquair Juwelier, The Hague, The Netherlands

98 Léopold Gautrait (zugeschrieben), Léon Gariod, Paris (Ausführung?), Anhänger/Brosche mit byzantinischer Frauenbüste, um 1900–1905, Gold, Email, Diamanten, Smaragde, Perle, 6,8 (mit Pendentif) × 4,6 cm. Léopold Gautrait (attributed to), Léon Gariod, Paris (made?), pendant/brooch with Byzantine woman's bust, *c.*1900–1905, gold, enamel, diamonds, emeralds, pearl, 6.8 (with pendentive) × 4.6 cm. Hessisches Landesmuseum, Darmstadt, Inv. MV 61:2

99 Brosche *Sarah Bernhardt*, nach einem Plakatentwurf von Alfons Mucha (früher Mucha/Fouquet zugeschrieben), nach 1897, Gold, Silber, Email, Diamanten, Rubin, Saphir, Perle, 5,8 × 4 cm. *Sarah Bernhardt* brooch, after a poster design by Alfons Mucha (previously attributed to Mucha/Fouquet), after 1897, gold, silver, enamel, diamonds, ruby, sapphire, pearl, 5.8 cm × 4 cm.
Hessisches Landesmuseum, Darmstadt, Inv. Kg 63:C100

101 Frédéric Boucheron, Krawattennadel mit Sonne und Mond, Paris, um 1880, zweischichtiger Karneol, Gold, Silber, Diamanten in Rosenschliff, 11 cm (Gesamtlänge). Frédéric Boucheron, tie pin with sun and moon, Paris, c.1880, carnelian cameo, gold, silver, rose-cut diamonds, 11 cm (total length). Les Arts décoratifs - Musée des Arts décoratifs, Paris, Département Art Nouveau / Art Déco, Paris, Inv. 28878 B

100 Alphonse Mucha, Plakat *Sarah Bernhardt (1844–1923)*, *La Plume*, 1896, Farblithografie, 75 × 55,5 cm.
Alphonse Mucha, *Sarah Bernhardt (1844-1923)* poster, *La Plume*, 1896, colour lithograph, 75 × 55.5 cm

sage lauten: Die Sonne gibt durch ihr Licht und ihre Wärme dem Menschen und aller Natur die Kraft, die das Leben auf dieser Erde erst ermöglicht (Abb. 97).

Dass die Sonne mit ihrer Symbolkraft zudem wirkungsvoll in der Schmuckwerbung eingesetzt wurde, zeigt ein Plakat der Pariser Juweliere Crespin & Dufayel aus der Zeit um 1900. Auf charmante Weise wird dort für *La Bague Soleil, Enrichie d'un Brillant* und die dazu passenden *Boucles d'Oreilles Soleil* Reklame gemacht.[64]

Sterne und Mondsicheln

Léopold Gautrait beschäftigte sich nicht nur mit der Sonne, sondern auch mit dem Motiv des Sterns – etwa in einem von ihm geschaffenen Halsschmuck. Als markantes Glied verbindet ein Stern den Anhänger mit der Kette, die das Schmuckstück hält (Abb. 98). Der Anhänger erinnert an eine Bronzebüste von Alphonse Mucha. Auch ein Plakat von Mucha, das die skandalumwitterte französische Schauspielerin Sarah Bernhardt mit einem Sterndiadem zeigt, diente offenbar als Vorbild für ein Schmuckstück: eine Brosche mit dem Porträt der Bernhardt, die um 1900 möglicherweise im Atelier von Georges Fouquet in Paris entstanden ist (Abb. 99, 100).

Auch der Pariser Schmuckkünstler Antoine Bricteux schuf einen Art-Nouveau-Anhänger mit Sternmotiv. Der darauf dargestellte Engel trägt ein Sternenkleid

102 Krawattennadel, Paris, 1904, Gold, Diamanten. Tie pin, Paris, 1904, gold, diamonds. Schmuckmuseum Pforzheim, Inv. KV 1531

und hält mit erhobenen Händen einen Diamantstern über seinem Haupt.⁶⁵ Wohl ebenfalls aus Paris stammt zudem eine kleine Krawattennadel aus Gold mit einer zierlichen unbekleideten Mädchengestalt. Sie trägt einen Diamantstern auf dem Kopf und einen weiteren in der Hand (Abb. 102).

Nächtliche Stimmung vermittelt ein um 1900 in Moskau entstandener Anhänger: Er zeigt ein von Mond und Sternen beschienenes russisches Dorf.⁶⁶ Ganz anders, nämlich durch die Kombination von Fledermäusen und Sternen, wird die Nacht hingegen in einem *bracelet de cheville* von René Lalique symbolisiert (Abb. 103). Eine Allegorie der Morgenröte findet sich auf einem Haarstecker des Pariser Hauses Vever: Ein geflügeltes Aktfigürchen aus Elfenbein schwebt über einer diamantbesetzten Mondsichel (Abb. 104). Insgesamt scheint der Mond im Schmuck des Art Nouveau allerdings keine allzu wichtige Rolle gespielt zu haben.

Wenn auch im Art Nouveau die ornamental verwandelten Bilder des Menschen, der Tiere und der Pflanzen als Gestaltungselemente vorrangig waren, so haben die Gestirne auch in dieser künstlerischen Bewegung eine nicht zu übersehende – vielleicht sogar romantische – Rolle gespielt.

103 René Lalique, Fußkettchen *Fledermaus*, Paris, um 1898/99, Gold, Transluzidemail, Diamanten, Opale, H 5,5 cm, L 20 cm. René Lalique, ankle chain *Bat*, Paris, c.1898/99, gold, translucent enamel, diamonds, opals, H 5.5, L 20 cm. Les Arts décoratifs – Musée des Arts décoratifs, Paris, Département Art Nouveau / Art Déco, Paris, Inv. 40100

for advertising jewellery. On it *La Bague Soleil, Enrichie d'un Brillant* [Sun ring, embellished with a brilliant-cut diamond] and matching *Boucles d'Oreilles Soleil* [Sun earrings] are promoted with charm.[64]

Stars and crescent moon

Léopold Gautrait not only worked with the sun motif but also with stars – for instance, in a piece of neck jewellery he created. A star is the stunning eye-catcher that links the pendant with the chain that holds the piece of jewellery (Fig. 98). The pendant is reminiscent of a bronze bust by Alphonse Mucha. A poster by Mucha featuring the actress Sarah Bernhardt, who lived and breathed scandal, wearing a star diadem evidently served as the model for a piece of jewellery: a brooch with a portrait of the Divine Sarah, which may have been made in Georges Fouquet's Paris studio c.1900 (Figs. 99, 100).

Another Paris artist-jeweller, Antoine Bricteux, created an Art Nouveau pendant with the star motif. The angel represented on it wears a starry garment and holds a diamond star above his head.[65] Moreover, a small gold cravat pin, probably also from Paris, features the graceful figure of a nude girl. The only thing she is wearing is a diamond star on her head and she carries another in her hand (Fig. 102).

A nocturnal mood is conveyed by a pendant made in Moscow c.1900: it shows a Russian village by the light of the moon and stars.[66] The night is symbolised in an entirely different way by a combination of bats and stars on a *bracelet de cheville* [anklet] by René Lalique (Fig. 103). An allegory of the first flush of dawn is the theme of a hairpin from Maison Vever in Paris: a tiny nude winged ivory figure hovers above a crescent moon set with diamonds (Fig. 104). On the whole, however, the moon does not seem to have played a particularly important role in Art Nouveau jewellery.

Although decoratively transfigured images of human beings, flora and fauna had priority in Art Nouveau, the heavenly bodies played a role – possibly even a romantic one – that was not negligible in this art movement as well.

104 Henri und Paul Vever, Haarstecker, Paris, 1905, Schildpatt, Elfenbein, Diamanten, Gold, Email. Henri and Paul Vever, hairpin, Paris, 1905, tortoiseshell, ivory, diamonds, gold, enamel. Alain Boucheron Collection

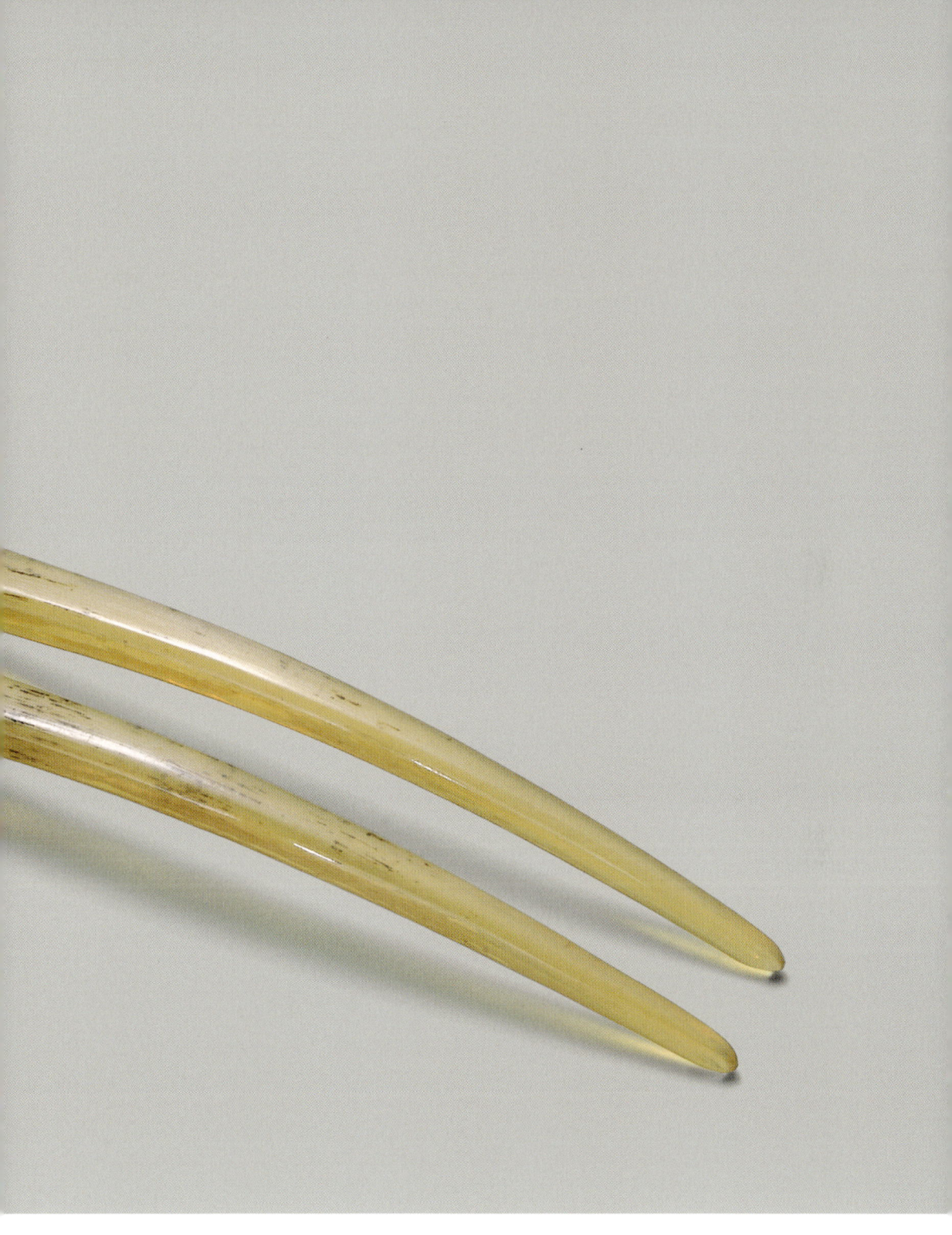

20. UND 21. JAHRHUNDERT

„In der Vergangenheit war Schmuck zuerst und vorrangig eine Angelegenheit des Designs […]. Mein Schmuck dagegen repräsentiert vor allem eine Idee! Ich wollte die Frauen überhäufen mit Konstellationen. Mit Sternen! Mit Sternen in allen Dimensionen, damit sie in ihren Haaren leuchten, in ganzen Bündeln, und mit Mondsicheln! Seht diese Kometen, deren Häupter auf der Schulter leuchten, deren funkelnde Schweife hinter die Schultern gleiten, um in einem Sternenregen zurückzufallen auf die Brust …" So äußerte sich Gabrielle Chanel in einem Gespräch mit A. de Gobart, das am 26. Oktober 1932 in der Pariser Tageszeitung *L'Intransigeant* veröffentlicht wurde. Und de Gobart erwähnt auch „die romantische Anmut dieser Konstellationen im Haar und über den Schultern der wächsernen Mannequins" (an denen die Schmuckstücke in Gabrielle Chanels Schmuckpräsentation gezeigt wurden).[67]

Zugegeben, diese Worte mögen heute etwas überzogen klingen und vielleicht auch nicht mehr ganz richtig erscheinen. Und dennoch trafen sie exakt die Stimmung und den Geist der Zeit, als die revolutionäre Modeschöpferin im November 1932 in ihrem Palais in der Rue du Faubourg Saint-Honoré ihre Aufsehen erregende Kollektion *Bijoux de Diamants* vorstellte (Abb. 105). Nach Gabrielle Chanels eigenen Aussagen spielten die Gestirne für sie seit ihrer Kindheit eine wichtige Rolle, was wohl ein Grund dafür war, dass sich die Diamantschmuck-Kollektion zwar nicht ausschließlich, aber doch vorrangig mit Sonne, Mond und Sternen befasste.[68]

Schon einige Zeit vor der Präsentation ihrer himmlischen Kollektion war Gabrielle Chanel der Italiener Fulco Santo Stefano della Cerda, Herzog von Verdura, vorgestellt worden. Von November 1933 bis Januar 1934 trug er als Chefdesigner für den Schmuck des Hauses Chanel Verantwortung. 1934 siedelte er in die Vereinigten Staaten von Amerika über. Dort kam es – zunächst in New York und anschließend in Hollywood – zu einer Zusammenarbeit mit Paul Flato, einem amerikanischen Juwelier, der für Marlene Dietrich, Greta Garbo, Rita Hayworth und andere Filmdiven tätig war. Möglicherweise wäre Flatos Armband *Shooting Star* von 1936 mit seinen 32 diamantbesetzten Sternen ohne die Mitarbeit von di Verdura nicht entstanden.[69] Mit Sicherheit ist di Verdura aber Autor einer *Plejaden*-Brosche aus dem Jahr 1946. Sie thematisiert mit Diamanten und je einem Saphircabochon in der Mitte die sieben Sterne dieser Konstellation.[70]

Auch andere Schmuckstücke sind ohne Kenntnis der Chanel-Kreationen des Jahres 1932 kaum denkbar, etwa ein 1935 entworfenes Schulterornament von

105　Chanel, Halsschmuck *Comète*, 1993, Neuauflage des von Gabrielle Chanel 1932 entworfenen Halsschmucks für ihre Serie *Bijoux de Diamants*, Platin, Diamanten. Chanel, *Comète* necklace, new edition of the necklace created by Gabrielle Chanel for her *Bijoux de Diamants* in 1932, platinum, diamonds. CHANEL Joaillerie

106   Juwelier Leicht, Brosche *Stern*, Pforzheim, 1996, Gelbgold, Weißgold, Diamanten. 1996 mit dem De Beers Diamonds International Award ausgezeichnet. Leicht Jewellers, *Star* brooch, Pforzheim, 1996, yellow gold, white gold, diamonds, awarded the De Beers Diamonds International Award in 1996.

TWENTIETH AND TWENTY-FIRST CENTURIES

'In the past jewellery was first and foremost a question of design. My jewellery, on the other hand, represents an idea above all! ... I wanted to cover women in constellations. In stars! In stars of all sizes and shapes to twinkle in their hair, fringes, crescent moons. Look at these comets, whose heads will sparkle on a shoulder and whose glittering tails will glide behind shoulders only to fall again in a rain of stars on the breast ...' Thus Gabrielle Chanel in the Paris daily *L'Intransigeant* on 26 October 1932 with A. de Gobart. And her interviewer went on to comment on 'the romantic grace of these constellations scattered in the hair and on the shoulders of these wax mannequins [...]. The jewellery has given work to a host of artists of merit.'[67]

Admittedly, all those effusive outpourings may sound rather gushy nowadays and may perhaps no longer appear quite justified. Yet the tone and style exactly matched the mood and spirit of the times when the revolutionary fashion designer presented her sensational collection *Bijoux de Diamants* at her palais in the rue du Faubourg Saint-Honoré in November 1932 (Fig. 105). As Gabrielle Chanel said herself, the heavenly bodies had played an important role for her since her childhood, which was probably one reason why the diamond jewellery collection was thematically, albeit not exclusively, based on the sun, moon and stars.[68]

Some time before she launched her heavenly collection, Gabrielle Chanel had been introduced to Fulco Santo Stefano della Cerda, Duke of Verdura. From November 1933 until January 1934 he was the head jewellery designer at Chanel. In 1934 Fulco di Verdura moved to the United States of America. There he collaborated – at first in New York, later in Hollywood – with Paul Flato, an American jeweller who worked for Marlene Dietrich, Greta Garbo, Rita Hayworth and other legendary film divas. Flato's *Shooting Star* bracelet (1936) featuring thirty-two stars set with diamonds might not have even seen the light of day without di Verdura's active collaboration.[69] A *Pleiades* brooch dating from 1946 is, however, definitely by di Verdura. The seven stars of this constellation are showcased thematically with diamonds and a cabochon sapphire at the centre of each.[70]

Other pieces of jewellery would also be unthinkable without their creators' knowledge of the 1932 Chanel collection – for instance, a shoulder ornament designed in 1935 by Suzanne Belperron, who worked for the renowned Paris jeweller René Boivin from 1919 until 1932. Made of platinum and set with diamonds, it features twenty-two stars.[71] However, goldsmiths and jewellers have on principle frequently reverted to cosmic motifs in the twentieth and twenty-first centuries. At Cartier (Jean Cocteau visualised Cartier in 1920 as a 'cunning magician who can capture scraps of moonlight against a gold thread of sunlight'[72]) a superb sunburst diadem was created in 1920.[73] The Paris studios of Van Cleef & Arpels launched a demi-parure, consisting of a pair of earrings and a brooch, entitled *Météore* in 1958.[74] And the Pforzheim jeweller Leicht won the De Beers Diamonds International Award in 1996 for a star piece (Fig. 106).

107 André Ribeiro, Armreif, um 2008, Kautschuk, Diamanten. André Ribeiro, bracelet, c.2008, natural rubber, diamonds

Suzanne Belperron, die von 1919 bis 1932 für den renommierten Pariser Juwelier René Boivin tätig war. Es besteht aus Platin mit Diamanten und zeigt 22 Sterne.[71] Aber auch ganz grundsätzlich nahmen sich die Goldschmiede und Juweliere des 20. und 21. Jahrhunderts immer wieder kosmischer Motive an. Bei Cartier (Jean Cocteau sah ihn als Magier, der den zerborstenen Mond in gesponnen Goldfäden einfängt[72]) wurde 1920 ein großartiges *Sunburst*-Diadem geschaffen.[73] In den Ateliers von Van Cleef & Arpels in Paris entstand 1958 eine Demi-Parure mit dem Titel *Météore*.[74] Und der Pforzheimer Juwelier Leicht gewann 1996 mit einem Sternschmuckstück den De Beers Diamonds International Award (Abb. 106).

The trend towards cosmic jewellery motifs has continued on into the early twenty-first century without a break. The diamonds set in André Ribeiro's rings and bangles of black rubber can be interpreted as stars shining in a dark night sky (Fig. 107). And the French designer Elie Top, who started out working for Yves Saint Laurent, developed a jewellery collection of his own entitled *Mécaniques Célestes* in 2015.

Jewellery by famous painters

Goldsmiths and jewellers were not the only ones to design jewellery. Famous painters often produced jewellery designs. The best known painter to do so is definitely Georges Braque. In the early 1960s he designed pieces of jewellery that attracted a great deal of attention worldwide and became coveted collector's items. Those brooches, pieces of neck jewellery and *objets de vitrine* were usually made after Braque's gouache design drawings by the goldsmith Heger de Loewenfeld. The pieces often feature bird motifs with a mythological frame of reference. However, the heavenly bodies were also part of the discussion – crescent moons, for instance, which were used as a motif for cufflinks. A particularly interesting piece is a rhodochrosite disc on which Braque placed a star set with diamonds. Here the cosmic motif draws on Greek mythology. The Hyades, daughters of Atlas, who carried the heavens in the form of the celestial sphere on his shoulders, were water nymphs. After the death of their brother Hyas, they were placed in the sky by the Olympian gods as stars associated with the spring rains.[75]

A gold disc by Max Ernst is dated to 1959. Although it is tersely called *Kopf* [*Head*], it represents a sun.[76] And one of Jean Lurçat's designs from the 1960s is a brooch, *Lune Visage* [*Moon Face*], a highly idiosyncratic interpretation of the moon motif (Fig. 108).

Art jewellery since the 1950s

Since the late 1950s artists in jewellery have been devoting themselves to the heavenly bodies for a wide variety of reasons in Germany, the United Kingdom, Italy, the Soviet Union and Russia, Switzerland, Spain, Israel, Japan, the United States and many other countries. Many of Giovanni Corvaja's delicate brooches may have been inspired by the rays of the sun.[77] *Rays of the Sun* is, in fact, the title of a 1989 brooch by Wendy Ramshaw.[78] Neck jewellery made of wood by Dorothea Prühl is succinctly called *Stern* [*Star*] by its creator (Fig. 109). Another piece of neck jewellery by this artist is entirely devoted to the *Mond* [*Moon*] (Fig. 110). And Tasso Mattar has combined a dromedary carved from a piece of bovine bone with a stainless-steel crescent moon set in gold to make a charming piece of jewellery (Fig. 111).

The purely formal aspect is given priority, it would seem, in the gold stars set with diamonds made by Günter Krauss,[79] and Therese Hilbert's three-dimensional silver star pendant is so convincing just because of its decorative character (Fig. 112). The brooches made by the Catalan artist Ramon Puig Cuyàs, in which the signs of the sky are combined with other attributes steeped in symbolism such as hearts and eyes, might plausibly lay claim to being not only decorative but also filled with magical content (Fig. 116). And as an artist working in jewellery in the Land of the Rising Sun, Wahei Ikezawa has created a brooch that deals with the national symbol of Japan (Fig. 113). A socially critical state-

Im beginnenden 21. Jahrhundert ist der Trend zum kosmischen Schmuckmotiv ungebrochen. So lassen sich die Diamanten auf André Ribeiros Ringen und Armreifen aus schwarzem Kautschuk als strahlende Sterne in dunkler Nacht deuten (Abb. 107). Und der Franzose Elie Top, der zuvor bei Yves Saint Laurent tätig war, entwickelte 2015 eine eigene Schmuckkollektion mit dem Titel *Mécaniques Célestes*.

Schmuck von bildenden Künstlern

Aber nicht nur Goldschmiede und Juweliere, auch bildende Künstler engagierten sich immer wieder als Entwerfer für Schmuck. Der in diesem Zusammenhang bekannteste ist zweifellos Georges Braque. In den frühen 1960er-Jahren schuf er Schmuckstücke, die international große Aufmerksamkeit erregten und zu gefragten Sammlerstücken wurden. Die Broschen, Halsschmuckstücke und Objets de Vitrine wurden meist nach Braques Gouache-Entwürfen von dem Goldschmied Heger de Loewenfeld ausgeführt. Oft handelte es sich um Vogelmotive mit mythologischen Bezügen. Aber auch die Gestirne waren Teil der Auseinandersetzung – etwa Mondsicheln, die als Motiv für Manschettenknöpfe dienten. Besonders interessant ist eine Scheibe aus Rhodocrosit, auf die Braque einen mit Diamanten besetzten Stern platzierte. Das kosmische Motiv bezieht sich hier auf die griechische Mythologie. Die Hyaden, Töchter von Atlas, dem Träger des Firmaments, waren Quellnymphen und wurden nach dem Tode ihres Bruders Hyas von den olympischen Göttern als Sterne in den Himmel gesetzt.[75]

Von Max Ernst stammt eine in das Jahr 1959 datierte goldene Scheibe. Obwohl sie lapidar *Kopf* genannt wird, stellt sie eine Sonne dar.[76] Und Jean Lurçat entwarf in den 1960er-Jahren unter anderem die Brosche *Lune Visage*, eine sehr eigenwillige Interpretation des Mondmotivs (Abb. 108).

Schmuckkunst seit den 1950er-Jahren

Seit den späten 1950er-Jahren widmeten sich Schmuckkünstler in Deutschland, Großbritannien, Italien, Russland, in der Schweiz, in Spanien, Israel, Japan, den USA und in vielen anderen Ländern aus ganz unterschiedlichen Motivationen heraus den Himmelskörpern. Manche der zarten Broschen von Giovanni Corvaja etwa mögen von Sonnenstrahlen angeregt worden sein.[77] *Rays of the Sun* lautet auch der Titel einer Brosche von Wendy Ramshaw aus dem Jahr 1989.[78] Von Dorothea Prühl stammt ein Halsschmuck aus Holz, den sie lapidar *Stern* nennt (Abb. 109). Ein weiterer Halsschmuck der Künstlerin ist voll und ganz dem *Mond* gewidmet (Abb. 110). Und Tasso Mattar kombiniert auf charmante Weise ein aus Rinderknochen geschnitztes Dromedar mit einer goldgefassten Mondsichel aus Edelstahl (Abb. 111). Die rein formale Komponente steht wohl bei den goldenen, mit Diamanten besetz-

108 Jean Lurçat (Entwurf), Gilbert Albert (Goldschmied), ausgeführt für Patek Philippe, Brosche *Lune Visage* (Mond-Gesicht), 1960/1966, Gold, zwei Perlen, H 6,6 cm, L 5,7 cm. Jean Lurçat (design), Gilbert Albert (goldsmith), made for Patek Philippe, brooch *Lune Visage* (Moon Face), 1960/1966, gold, two pearls, H 6.6 cm, L 5.7 cm. Les Arts décoratifs – Musée des Arts décoratifs, Paris, Département des Bijoux, Inv. 2003.125.14

ment can, on the other hand, probably be imputed to *Sick Moon*, a brooch made by American artists Robin Kranitzky and Kim Overstreet. It seems to be full of murky allusions to drug problems and other dangers to life (Fig. 114).

Many artists in jewellery have been inspired by ancient mythologies, music, the visual arts and also astronomical events such as eclipses of the sun and moon. In a 1992 brooch from his *Mito* cycle, Bruno Martinazzi, who has frequently investigated antiquity in his work, alludes to the Greek personification of the sun, Helios, who was worshipped as a god, interpretations of whom range from the Colossus of Rhodes to the New York Statue of Liberty. 'Lady Liberty' also appears in *Une Semaine à New York* [*A Week in New York*], a brooch by Sabine Finkbeiner,[80] and in a piece of jewellery by Gijs Bakker, which was made as a tribute to Madeleine K. Albright under the auspices of *Brooching It Diplomatically*, a 1998 exhibition project initiated by Helen W. Drutt English (Fig. 115).

Links with music are encountered in the work of Kevin Coates, to take one example. He studied Mozart's *Magic Flute* intensively, quoting this opera in *Entry of the Queen of the Night* (1996), a tiara which can also be worn at the neck (Fig. 117). He may even be indirectly alluding to the 1812 Schinkel stage set with the crescent moon on the tiara (Fig. 14).[81]

109 Dorothea Prühl, Halsschmuck *Stern*, 1999, Kirschholz, H 6 cm. Dorothea Prühl, *Star* neckpiece, 1999, cherry wood, H 6 cm

110 Dorothea Prühl, Halsschmuck *Mond*, 2003, Titan, Gold, L 34 cm. Dorothea Prühl, *Moon* neckpiece, 2003, titanium, gold, L 34 cm

111 Tasso Mattar, Brosche *Dromedar im Mondschein*, 2000, Knochen, Gold, Perlmutt, Privatsammlung. Tasso Mattar, *Dromedary by Moonlight* brooch, 2000, bone, gold, mother-of-pearl, private collection

112 Therese Hilbert, Anhänger *Stern*, 1986, Silber. Therese Hilbert, *Star* pendant, 1986, silver. Schmuckmuseum Pforzheim, Inv. ifa 24

ten Sternen von Günter Krauss im Vordergrund,[79] und auch Therese Hilberts dreidimensionaler silberner Sternanhänger überzeugt vorwiegend dank seines dekorativen Charakters (Abb. 112). Die Broschen des Katalanen Ramon Puig Cuyàs, in denen die Zeichen des Himmels mit anderen symbolträchtigen Attributen wie Herzen und Augen kombiniert sind, dürfen sicherlich den Anspruch erheben, nicht nur dekorativ, sondern voller magischer Inhalte zu sein (Abb. 116). Und der Japaner Wahei Ikezawa schuf – als Schmuckkünstler im Land der aufgehenden Sonne – eine Brosche, die sich mit dem Landessymbol beschäftigt (Abb. 113). Eine eher gesellschaftskritische Aussage hingegen darf man wohl der Brosche *Sick Moon* zuschreiben, die von den Amerikanern Robin Kranitzky und Kim Overstreet stammt. Sie scheint voller düsterer Anspielungen auf Drogenprobleme und andere Gefährdungen des Lebens zu sein (Abb. 114).

Viele Schmuckkünstler ließen und lassen sich von alten Mythologien, von Musik und bildender Kunst sowie von astronomischen Ereignissen wie den Sonnen- und Mondfinsternissen anregen. So nimmt Bruno Martinazzi, der sich in seinem Schaffen immer wieder mit der Antike auseinandersetzt, in einer 1992

113 Wahei Ikezawa, Brosche, 1982, Gold, Kupfer, Messing, Silber. Wahei Ikezawa, brooch, 1982, gold, copper, brass, silver.
Schmuckmuseum Pforzheim, Inv. 1984/10

114 Robin Kranitzky, Kim Overstreet, Brosche *Kranker Mond*, 1989, Balsaholz, Azetat, Silber, Kunststoff, Postkartenfragmente, Fundstücke, 7,6 × 8,2 × 1,3 cm, Privatsammlung. Robin Kranitzky, Kim Overstreet, *Sick Moon* brooch, 1989, balsa wood, acetate, silver, plastics, fragments of postcards, found objects, 7.6 × 8.2 × 1.3 cm, private collection

115 Gijs Bakker, Brosche *Liberty*, entworfen 1997, ausgeführt 2002, Silber, Uhren aus dem Handel, 9,8 × 11,4 cm. Gijs Bakker, *Liberty* brooch, designed 1997, made 2002, silver, commercial watches, 9.7 × 11.4 cm. The Museum of Fine Arts, Houston, Helen Williams Drutt Collection, gift of Helen Williams Drutt English, Inv. 2002.3614

entstandenen Brosche aus dem *Mito*-Zyklus auf den griechischen Sonnengott Helios Bezug, dessen Bedeutung vom Koloss von Rhodos bis zur Freiheitsstatue reicht. „Lady Liberty" erscheint auch in der Brosche *Une Semaine à New York* von Sabine Finkbeiner[80] und in einem Schmuckstück von Gijs Bakker, das im Rahmen des 1998 von Helen Williams Drutt English initiierten Projektes *Brooching It Diplomatically* für Madeleine K. Albright entstand (Abb. 115).

Bezüge zur Musik finden sich etwa bei Kevin Coates. Er setzte sich intensiv mit Mozarts Zauberflöte auseinander und zitiert diese Oper in seinem 1997 entstandenen Kopfschmuck *Entry of the Queen of the Night* (Abb. 117). Mit der darin gezeigten Mondsichel verweist er möglicherweise sogar indirekt auf Schinkels Bühnenbild von 1815 (Abb. 14).[81]

116 Ramon Puig Cuyàs, Brosche *Carmen*, 1996, Silber, Alpaka, Kunststoff, Acrylfarbe. Ramon Puig Cuyàs, *Carmen* brooch, 1996, silver, German silver, plastic, acrylic paint. Schmuckmuseum Pforzheim, Inv. 1999/14

117 Kevin Coates, Diadem/Halsschmuck *Auftritt der Königin der Nacht* (Mozart-Serie), 1996, Gelbgold, Weißgold, Silber, Mondstein, Opal, Labradorit, Perlmutt, Blattgold, H 12 cm, L 20 cm, B 16 cm. Kevin Coates, tiara/neckpiece *Entry of the Queen of the Night* (Mozart series), 1996, yellow gold, white gold, silver, moonstone, opal, labradorite, mother-of-pearl, gold leaf, H 12 cm, L 20 cm, W 16 cm. National Museums Scotland, Inv. K.1999.267

118 Rolf Elsässer, Brosche, 1999, Gold, geschwärzter Stahl, Brillant.
Rolf Elsässer, brooch, 1999, gold, blackened steel, brilliant-cut diamond

119 Wilhelm Buchert, Armschmuck, 1969, Gold, Opal, Perle. Wilhelm Buchert, bracelet, 1969, gold, opal, pearl.
Schmuckmuseum Pforzheim, Inv. 1969/112

120 Peter Skubic, Brosche *Sonnenfinsternis*, 2000, Gold, Silber, Niello, Dm 5 cm, Privatsammlung. Peter Skubic, *Solar Eclipse* brooch, 2000, gold, silver, niello, dia. 5 cm, private collection

121 Mark Baldin, Ring *Kosmos*, 2015, Silber, Gold, Diamanten, blauer und gelber Saphir. Mark Baldin, *Cosmos* ring, 2015, silver, gold diamonds, blue and yellow sapphire

122 Juri Bylkov, Ring *Sphären*, St. Petersburg, 2015, Titanium, Privatsammlung. Juri Bylkov, *Spheres* ring, St Petersburg, 2015, titanium, private collection

Peter Skubic wiederum nahm die Sonnenfinsternis von 1999 zum Anlass, eine ebenso benannte Brosche zu schaffen (Abb. 120). Die Pforzheimer Goldschmiedezunft „Schmuck + Gestaltung" ließ sich von dem Ereignis ebenfalls inspirieren. Sie schrieb für ihre Mitglieder einen Wettbewerb aus, dessen Ziel es war, die Sonnenfinsternis künstlerisch in Schmuck umzusetzen (Abb. 118). Auch Bernhard Schobinger, der sich seit den 1980er-Jahren schon mehrfach mit den Gestirnen befasst hatte, schuf 1989 einen Halsschmuck mit dem Titel *Sonnenfinsternis* (Abb. 123). Er kommentiert ihn mit den Worten: „Die Sonne umkreist den Hals. Es könnte aber ebenso gut der Mond sein; die Idee demonstriert Himmelsmechanik, Zunehmen und Abnehmen, bei der Sonne als Phasen einer Finsternis." Andere Schmuckstücke von Schobinger, die sich mit den Himmelskörpern befassen, tragen Titel wie *Sonnensäge*, *Sonnenscheibe*, *Sonnenrad*, *Sonne – Mond* oder *Ring among Stars*.[82]

Auf andere Weise werden astronomische Zusammenhänge in Wilhelm Bucherts Armreif von 1969 thematisiert. Hier sind Erde und Mond wie in einem kleinen Planetarium um die Sonne herum angeordnet (Abb. 119). Auch Giampaolo Babetto schuf einen Armreif, der ähnlich wie die astronomischen Faltringe der Barockzeit (s. Abb. 56) die Umlaufbahnen der Sterne symbolisieren könnte. Und auch die in den 1970er-Jahren entstandenen Broschen von Gerhard Rothmann und Fritz Maierhofer haben das Universum zum Inhalt.[83] Den Kosmos als Ganzen untersuchen Juri

123 Bernhard Schobinger, Halsschmuck *Sonnenfinsternis*, 1989, Gelbgold, Email, Privatsammlung. Bernhard Schobinger, *Solar Eclipse* neckpiece, 1989, yellow gold, enamel, private collection

Peter Skubic, on the other hand, took the 1999 solar eclipse as his starting point for creating a brooch of that name (Fig. 120). The Pforzheim goldsmiths' guild Schmuck + Gestaltung [Jewellery + Design] was also inspired by the celestial event. It organised a competition for their members with the aim of translating the solar eclipse into jewellery (Fig. 118). The Swiss jewellery maker Bernhard Schobinger, who has been preoccupied with the heavenly bodies on several occasions since the 1980s, also made a necklace entitled *Sonnenfinsternis* [*Solar Eclipse*] (Fig. 123). His comment on it is as follows: 'The sun orbits about the neck.

124　Attai Chen, Anhänger *Kalaschnikow*, 2008, Holz, Nylon,
8 × 8 × 0,5 cm. Attai Chen, *Kalashnikov* pendant, 2008, wood, nylon,
8 × 8 × 0.5 cm

Bylkov aus Sankt Petersburg (Abb. 122) und Mark Baldin aus Jekaterinburg (Abb. 121).

Völlig anders waren die Voraussetzungen, die in der jungen Schmuckszene Israels zur Auseinandersetzung mit dem Motiv des Sterns führten. Aggressiv und provozierend ist Attai Chens Anhänger *Kalaschnikov* (2008), der auf die unselige Verquickung von Gewalt und dem Davidstern (*Magen David*) hinweist (Abb. 124). Zoya Cherkasskys Brosche *Jude* (2001/02) erinnert reflektierend und anklagend an den „Judenstern", den die Europäer jüdischer Abstammung während der Nazi-Diktatur in Deutschland und in den von Deutschland besetzten Ländern tragen mussten (Abb. 125). Die Erinnerung an diese dunkle Zeit dürfte auch bei dem Anhänger *Holiness* (2011) von Deganit Stern Schocken eine Rolle spielen.[84]

125 Zoya Cherkassky, Brosche *Jude* (Edition von 18), 2001/02, 18 kt Gold, 5 × 5 cm. Zoya Cherkassky, *Jude* brooch (edition of 18), 2001/02, 18 ct gold, 5 × 5 cm.
Courtesy of Rosenfeld Gallery, Tel Aviv

It could, however, just as well be the moon; the idea demonstrates celestial mechanics, waxing and waning, with the sun as phases of an eclipse.' Other pieces of jewellery by Schobinger which have to do with the heavenly bodies boast titles such as *Sonnensäge* [*Sun Saw*], *Sonnenscheibe* [*Sun Disc*], *Sonnenrad* [*Sun Wheel*], *Sonne – Mond* [*Sun – Moon*], and *Ring among Stars*.[82]

Astronomical associations are the theme of a Wilhelm Buchert bangle (1969) but presented in in a different way. Here the earth and the moon are arranged about the sun as if in a minuscule planetarium (Fig. 119). Giampaolo Babetto also created a bangle that might symbolise the orbits of stars in a star system in a way similar to the folding astronomical rings of the Baroque era (see Fig. 56). And brooches made by Gerhard Rothmann and Fritz Maierhofer in the 1970s are also about the universe.[83] Juri Bylkov from Saint Petersburg (Fig. 122) and Mark Baldin in Yekaterinburg investigated the cosmos as a whole (Fig. 121).

The investigation of the star motif by the young Israeli jewellery scene is premised on entirely different motives. Attai Chen's *Kalashnikov* (2008), a pendant which refers to the fatal fusion of violence and the Star of David (Hebrew: Magen David), is aggressive and provocative (Fig. 124). Zoya Cherkassky's brooch *Jude* [*Jew*] (2001/02) is a reflective and accusatory reminiscence of the *Judenstern*, the star-shaped yellow badge European Jews were forced to wear during the Nazi dictatorship in Germany and in the countries occupied by Nazi Germany (Fig. 125). Recollection of this dark era probably also plays a role in *Holiness* (2011), a pendant by Deganit Stern Schocken.[84]

126 Chopard, Anhänger *Happy Sun* aus der Serie *Happy Diamonds*, Weißgold, Brillanten. Chopard, pendant *Happy Sun* from the *Happy Diamonds* series, white gold, diamonds

Die Schmuckindustrie

Unzählig sind heute die Produzenten in aller Welt, die Schmuckstücke unter Verwendung kosmischer Motive herstellen – sei es als Luxusgut oder Modeschmuck, in limitierten oder großen Auflagen, in minderer oder höherer Qualität.

Die weltweit aktive deutsch-schweizerische Firma Chopard setzte in mehreren hochkarätigen Schmuck- und Uhrenkreationen (etwa in der *Happy-Diamonds*-Serie) der Sonne ein strahlendes Schmuck-Denkmal (Abb. 126). Ruppenthal in Idar-Oberstein beeindruckt mit seinen Kollierschließen im Planeten-Design (Abb. 127). Die Moskauer Schmuckmanufaktur Gevorgian stellt Fingerringe her, die den Nachthimmel aus Saphiren durch Diamantsterne symbolisieren. Und auch in den Schmuckkollektionen des mexikanischen Unternehmens Sergio Bustamante, das mit phantasievollen Kreationen auf sich aufmerksam macht, sind Sonne, Mond und Sterne wichtige Merkmale.

127   Ruppenthal, Kollier-Schließen im Planeten-Design, 2016, Gelbgold, Weißgold, Rotgold bzw. Rugatec mit Edelsteinvarianten. Ruppenthal, jewellery clasps in planet-type design, 2016, yellow gold, white gold, rose gold or Rugatec with gem stones

The jewellery industry

Countless producers worldwide are manufacturing pieces of jewellery using cosmic motifs – be they luxury articles or costume jewellery, in limited editions or mass-produced, low or high quality.

Chopard, a Swiss-German company, targets a global market. The sun has been radiantly celebrated in several sumptuous jewellery creations and jewelled watches – for instance, in the *Happy Diamond* series (Fig. 126). Ruppenthal in Idar-Oberstein has made an impact internationally with its interchangeable magnetic necklace clasps designed to look like planets (Fig. 127). Gevorgian, a Moscow jewellery manufacturer, makes finger rings paved with sapphires and diamond stars to symbolise the night sky. And the sun, moon and stars figure prominently in the jewellery collections launched by the Mexican company Sergio Bustamante, which has attracted attention with its imaginative creations.

Thus the heavenly bodies have become extremely successful jewellery motifs worldwide even though they are now largely without magical, mythological or

So sind die Gestirne global zu äußerst erfolgreichen Schmuckmotiven geworden, wenn auch nun weitgehend ohne magisch-mythologischen oder symbolischen Hintergrund. Selbst die bronzezeitliche Himmelsscheibe von Nebra kann damit in vereinfachter Form zum Schmuckanhänger werden – und feiert nach mehr als 3600 Jahren ein praktisch-dekoratives Comeback.

Berühmte Edelsteine

Ganz besondere Edelsteine, vornehmlich Diamanten, zeichnete man ihrer Bedeutung wegen mit klangvollen Namen aus, die nicht selten auf Himmelskörper anspielen. Berühmt wurde der tropfenförmige *Moon of Baroda*, ein seit Jahrhunderten bekannter gelber Diamant aus Indien. Er hatte eine Zeitlang den Habsburgern gehört und war nachweislich von Kaiserin Maria Theresia getragen worden. Der *Moon of Baroda* schmückte aber auch den Hals von Marilyn Monroe – sowohl bei der Tonaufnahme des Songs *Diamonds Are a Girl's Best Friend* als auch bei der Premiere des Films *Gentlemen Prefer Blondes*.[85]

Der größte jemals gefundene Diamant, der *Cullinan* (im Rohzustand wog er mehr als 3100 Karat), wurde 1908 in Amsterdam in neun große und zahllose kleinere Teile gespalten und geschliffen. Das größte dieser Stücke, der *Cullinan I*, erhielt den Beinamen *The Great Star of Africa*[86]; der *Cullinan II* wird auch *Lesser Star of Africa* genannt. Weitere „Stern"-Diamanten sind der *Star of Sierra Leone*, der *Star of South Africa* (nicht zu verwechseln mit den beiden aus dem *Cullinan* geschliffenen *Stars*), der vermutlich aus Indien stammende *Star of the East* sowie der 1853 in Brasilien gefundene *Star of the South*. Der sogenannte *Skull Star Diamond* befindet sich auf der Stirn der Skulptur *For the Love of God* (2007) von Damien Hirst.

1990 wurde im damaligen Zaire (heute: Demokratische Republik Kongo) der *De Beers Millennium Star* gefunden; mit mehr als 203 Karat (nach seiner Bearbeitung) ist er heute der zweitgrößte Top-Colour-Diamant der Welt. Der 1999 in Südafrika gefundene und nach dem Schliff 59,6 Karat schwere *Pink Star* schließlich war im November 2013 in Genf zur Auktion gekommen und für die Summe von mehr als 83 Millionen Dollar zugeschlagen worden. Der potenzielle Käufer konnte den Betrag allerdings vorläufig nicht aufbringen, so dass sich der Diamant nach wie vor im Bestand des Auktionshauses Sotheby's befindet.

Mond und Stern als Wertbegriffe? Zumindest im Zusammenhang mit berühmten und besonders kostbaren Edelsteinen ist dies sicher der Fall!

symbolic content. Even the Bronze Age Nebra sky disc has inspired contemporary pendants in more or less simplified form – thus celebrating a practical and decorative comeback after more than 3,600 years.

Famous precious stones
Very special precious stones, chiefly diamonds, are given resounding names because they are so important, and these names are often allusions to the heavenly bodies. The teardrop-shaped *Moon of Baroda* is a canary diamond from India that has been known for centuries. For a while it belonged to the Habsburg dynasty, and Empress Maria Theresia verifiably wore it. The *Moon of Baroda* also adorned Marilyn Monroe's neck – while she was recording the song 'Diamonds Are a Girl's Best Friend' and at the premiere of the film *Gentlemen Prefer Blondes*.[85]

The largest diamond ever found, the *Cullinan* (in the rough it weighed more than 3,100 carats), was split into nine large and numerous smaller stones and cut in Amsterdam in 1908. The largest of these stones, the *Cullinan I*, was given the epithet *The Great Star of Africa*;[86] the *Cullinan II* is also known as the *Lesser Star of Africa*. Other 'star' diamonds are the *Star of Sierra Leone*, the *Star of South Africa* (not to be confused with the two *Stars* cut from the *Cullinan*), the *Star of the East*, which presumably came from India, and the *Star of the South*, found in Brazil in 1853. The so-called *Skull Star Diamond* is on the forehead of Damien Hirst's diamond-set platinum cast of a human skull, *For the Love of God* (2007).

The *De Beers Millennium Star* was found in 1990 in what was then Zaire (now: the Democratic Republic of the Congo). Weighing more than 203 carats (after it was cut and polished), it is now the second largest top-colour diamond in the world. The *Pink Star*, found in South Africa in 1999, still weighed 59.6 carats after it had been cut and polished. It was put up for sale at auction in Geneva in November 2013 and sold for more than USD 83 million. The potential buyer, however, has still not been able to come up with the sum so the diamond has become part of the Sotheby's inventory.

The moon and stars as concepts of value? This is certainly the case in connection with celebrated and particularly valuable precious stones!

128 Fibel, Tunesien, frühes 20. Jh., Silber. Fibula, Tunisia, early 20th century, silver. Sammlung Ute Wittich

AUSSER-EUROPÄISCHE KULTUREN

Das vorliegende Buch setzt inhaltlich einen Schwerpunkt auf Europa und die westliche Welt. Es kann in diesem Kontext daher nur andeutungsweise auf die Gestirne im Schmuck außereuropäischer Kulturen hingewiesen werden, denn die Erscheinungsformen sind ausgesprochen vielfältig. Einige ausgewählte Schlaglichter allerdings mögen diese Vielfalt belegen.

129 Halsschmuck, Marokko, frühes 20. Jh., Silber, Bernstein, Privatsammlung. Neck jewellery, Morocco, early 20th century, silver, amber, private collection

130 Hals- und Brustschmuck, Marokko, 2. Hälfte 20. Jh., Korallen und Glassteine auf Leder. Neck and breast jewellery, Morocco, latter half of the 20th century, coral and glass stones on leather. Sammlung Herion, Pforzheim

131 Hochzeitskollier, Tunesien, Mitte 20. Jh., Silber, vergoldet.
Wedding necklace, Tunisia, mid-20th century, silver-gilt. Sammlung Ute Wittich

NON-EUROPEAN CULTURES

The content of the present book focuses chiefly on Europe and the Western world. Hence in this context the heavenly bodies in the jewellery of non-European cultures can only be touched on in passing since the relevant phenomena are definitely diverse in character. Nonetheless, a small selection of highlights may give some idea of this diversity.

The Arab world

From North Africa through the Arabian peninsula to Yemen: everywhere in the Islamic world jewellery has always been worn that is in the main associated with the moon and stars, although less so with the sun. The crescent moon, the symbol of Islam, and occasionally also the disc of the full moon appear individually or in clusters on countless pieces of jewellery – on necklaces (Fig. 129) and finger rings as well as fibulae, which are used to pin together the various parts of robes (Fig. 128).

Arabische Welt

Von Nordafrika über die arabische Halbinsel bis zum Jemen: Überall in der islamischen Welt wurden – und werden noch immer – Schmuckstücke getragen, die vornehmlich mit Monden und Sternen, weniger häufig dagegen mit der Sonne verbunden sind. Die Mondsichel, das Symbol des Islam, und gelegentlich auch die volle Mondscheibe erscheinen einzeln oder in mehreren Exemplaren auf zahllosen Schmuckstücken – auf Kolliers (Abb. 129) und Fingerringen ebenso wie auf Fibeln, die zum Zusammenstecken verschiedener Gewandteile dienen (Abb. 128).

In Marokko sind die prachtvollen Geschmeide der Berberfrauen vorherrschend, die meist aus Silber gefertigt und mit Email farbig verziert sind. Die Anhänger und Ketten mit den Mondsicheln können als Zeichen von Wohlstand ebenso dienen wie als religiöse Symbole. Außergewöhnlich und bisher ohne Parallele ist ein vermutlich aus dem Atlasgebirge stammender Hals- und Brustschmuck: Er setzt sich zusammen aus einer nach oben geöffneten Mondsichel und einer Sonnenscheibe; beide sind reich mit einfachen Schmucksteinen, Korallen und Glasperlen verziert (Abb. 130).

Zur Hochzeitsausstattung tunesischer Frauen gehören vielgliedrige Kolliers, sogenannte Dhiriy, deren wesentliche Merkmale silbervergoldete Mondsicheln sind (Abb. 131). Junge tunesische Männer hingegen schmücken sich oft mit Amulettanhängern, auf denen Mond und Stern vereinigt sind. Im Jemen schließlich wurden – und werden nach wie vor – silberne Amulettbehälter zur Aufnahme religiöser Texte getragen, die häufig mit Mond- und Sternmotiven verziert sind (Abb. 132).

Türkei, Kaukasus und Zentralasien

Zur islamischen Welt, in der der Mond im Schmuck stark verbreitet ist, gehören auch die Türkei sowie viele Länder, die einmal Teil des Osmanischen Reiches waren. Tierschmuck und osmanische Rüstungen waren zum Teil ebenfalls mit dem Mondmotiv ausgestattet. Darauf weisen unter anderem Zierbeschläge aus der sogenannten „Türkenbeute" hin (Abb. 133), die sich heute im Badischen Landesmuseum in Karlsruhe befindet. Der Grundstock dieser Bestände war von Markgraf Ludwig Wilhelm, genannt Türkenlouis, im 17. Jahrhundert in mehreren Schlachten errungen worden.

Der Kaukasus, das eurasische Hochgebirge zwischen dem Schwarzen und dem Kaspischen Meer, ist von mehr als fünfzig Bevölkerungsgruppen besiedelt, die sich überwiegend zum Islam bekennen. Naheliegend ist deshalb, dass beispielsweise in Dagestan mit seiner vorwiegend muslimischen Bevölkerung amulettartige Schmuckstücke mit Mondsicheln und Sternen bekannt und beliebt sind. Auch in Aserbaidschan, in Georgien und selbst bei den islamischen Kasan-Tartaren in

132 Amulettanhänger, Jemen, Mitte 20. Jh., Silber, Glassteine. Amulet pendant, Yemen, mid-20th century, silver, glass stones. Sammlung Herion, Pforzheim

133 Gehänge in Form eines Mondes, Zierbeschlag eines Reitzeugs, osmanisch, 2. Hälfte 17. Jh., Silber, Silberdraht, vergoldet. Pendant in the shape of a moon, decoration from riding gear, Ottoman, latter half of the 17th century, silver, silver-gilt wire. Badisches Landesmuseum Karlsruhe, Inv. D 149 a

Russland finden sich Schmuckstücke mit Monden und mit Sternen. Allerdings scheint nicht immer der Bezug zur Religion gegeben zu sein; auch das rein dekorative Element spielt hier wohl eine wichtige Rolle.[87]

In zentralasiatischen Ländern wie Kasachstan und Usbekistan, vor allem aber in Turkmenistan – dort bei den Tekke und den Yomud –, sind ebenfalls Schmuckstücke mit Sternmotiven bekannt und beliebt. Hervorzuheben ist in diesem Zusammenhang die sogenannte Gül-yaka. Diese runde, silbervergoldete Zierscheibe ist mit Karneolen beziehungsweise karneolfarbenen Glassteinen besetzt und wird von Frauen als Kragenschmuck getragen (Abb. 134).[88]

Südostasien und Indonesien

In Südchina, Nordthailand und in angrenzenden Regionen Südostasiens leben die Miao, eine Bevölkerungsgruppe, die für ihre äußerst bemerkenswerte Silberschmuckkultur bekannt ist. Die Frauen der Hmong, die in China zu den Miao gezählt werden, schmücken sich bei besonderen Festlichkeiten noch heute mit silbernen Scheiben, die sehr häufig einen vielstrahligen Stern in der Mitte tragen.

Indonesien, ein Staat, der über 17.500 große und kleine Inseln umfasst und dessen Territorium teils zu Asien, teils zu Australien gehört, ist zugleich das Land mit der weltweit größten islamischen Bevölkerung. Auch im Schmuck dieser Region spielen die Abbilder der Gestirne eine bedeutende Rolle. Einzelne Inseln haben dabei ihre jeweils eigenen Schmucktypen ausgebildet. So finden sich

In Morocco the splendid pieces worn by Berber women are the predominant form of jewellery. Most are made of silver and decorated with coloured enamel. Pendants and chains with crescent moons can serve as signs of wealth and as religious symbols. A large pectoral from the Atlas Mountains is exceptional and hitherto unparalleled: it is made up of a crescent moon pointing upwards and a sun disc, both of which are richly decorated with simple gem stones, pieces of coral and glass beads (Fig. 130).

Tunisian women's dowries include multi-strand chains, known as *dhiriy*. Silver-gilt crescent moons are their most notable feature (Fig. 131). Young Tunisian men, on the other hand, often adorn themselves with pendant amulets on which moon and stars are united. In Yemen silver amulet cases still worn today – as they were in the past – to hold religious texts are often decorated with moon and star motifs (Fig. 132).

134 Schmuckscheibe, Turkmenistan, 20. Jh., Silber, teilvergoldet, Glassteine. Ornamental disc, Turkmenistan, 20th century, parcel-gilt silver, glass stones. Sammlung Ute Wittich

135 Armreif *Lola-Lola*, Indonesien, Messing (?). *Lola-Lola* bracelet, Indonesia, brass (?). Privatsammlung, Pforzheim

beispielsweise auf Sumatra Schmuckstücke mit Sonnen, Monden und Sternen, wobei zumindest gelegentlich gewisse Einflüsse aus der islamischen Handwerkskunst nicht auszuschließen sind.[89] Von der Insel Sulawesi hingegen stammt ein großer und schwerer Armreif, ein *Lola-Lola*, der wohl zu Recht als ein Sonnensymbol gedeutet wird (Abb. 135).

Eine besonders reiche Schmuckkultur findet sich auf der Insel Flores. Zwar bekennen sich ihrer Bewohner – als Resultat einer von Niederländern und Portugiesen geprägten jahrhundertelangen Kolonialgeschichte – überwiegend zum Christentum. Doch scheinen weder die christliche Religion noch der Islam einen Einfluss auf den von Gold dominierten Schmuck der Insel gehabt zu haben. Vielmehr sind es jahrtausendealte Traditionen, die sich hier bis in die Gegenwart

Turkey, the Caucasus and central Asia

The Islamic world, in which the moon is so widespread in jewellery, also includes Turkey as well as many other countries that were once part of the Ottoman Empire. Some animal jewellery and Ottoman suits of armour were also decorated with the moon motif. This is attested by decorative mounts from what are called the *Türkenbeute* (Turkish spoils; Fig. 133), which are now in the Badisches Landesmuseum in Karlsruhe. The nucleus of these exhibits was taken by Ludwig Wilhelm, Margrave of Baden, dubbed 'Türkenlouis', at several battles in the seventeenth century.

The Caucasus, the mountainous Eurasian region between the Black Sea and the Caspian Sea, is settled by more than fifty ethnic groups, most of which profess Islam as their religion. Unsurprisingly, therefore, amulet-like pieces of jewellery with crescent moons and stars are known from Dagestan, for instance, where they are popular with the mainly Muslim population. In Azerbaijan, in Georgia, and even among the Muslim Kazan (Qazan) Tartars in Russia pieces of jewellery featuring moons and stars occur. However, the reference to religion does not always appear to be present; the purely decorative aspect probably plays an important role here as well.[87]

Pieces of jewellery with star motifs are known from central Asian countries such as Kazakhstan and Uzbekistan and especially Turkmenistan – among the Tekke and Yomud – and are popular there. A type of jewellery known as *Gül-yaka* should be emphasised in this connection. This is a round, silver-gilt decorative disc set with carnelian or, alternatively, with carnelian-coloured glass stones and is worn by women as a collar ornament (Fig. 134).[88]

South East Asia and Indonesia

Southern China, northern Thailand and neighbouring regions of South East Asia are home to the Miao, an ethnic group famous for their extraordinary, truly remarkable culture of silver jewellery. The women of the Hmong, who in China are classified as belonging to the Miao, still adorn themselves for important festivities with silver discs that often bear a multi-pointed star at the centre.

Indonesia, a country comprising more than 17,500 large and small islands and whose territory belongs geographically partly to Asia and in part to Australasia, is also the nation with the largest Muslim population worldwide. Representations of the heavenly bodies play an important role in the jewellery of this region, too. Individual islands have developed their own distinctive types of jewellery. Pieces of jewellery with sun, moon and stars occur on Sumatra, for instance; here the possibility of at least occasional influences from Islamic crafts cannot be eliminated.[89] A large, heavy bangle, a *Lola-Lola*, from the island of Sulawesi, on the other hand, is interpreted, probably rightly, as a sun symbol (Fig. 135).

The island of Flores boasts a particularly rich jewellery culture. A majority of the island's inhabitants profess Christianity – as a consequence of centuries of colonial history shaped by the Dutch and the Portuguese. Nevertheless, neither Christianity nor Islam seems to have exerted any influence on the jewellery of Flores, which is for the most part gold. On the contrary, traditions that go back thousands of years still resonate.[90] A pectoral designated a 'solar barge' in specialist publications is famous: a gold boat serves here as a symbol for the sun travelling through time and space. It is united with a sunburst to form an

136 Goldscheiben-Anhänger („Seelenscheibe"?), Ashanti-Region, Ghana, 19./20. Jh. (?), Gold, Fasern, Dm 21,5 cm. Gold disc pendant ('soul disc'?), Asante region, Ghana, 19th/20th century (?), gold, fibres, dia. 21.5 cm. British Museum, London, Inv. Af1925,1024.1

hinein auswirken.[90] Berühmt ist ein in der Literatur als *Sonnenbarke* bezeichnetes Pektorale: Ein goldenes Boot dient hier als Symbol für die Reise durch Zeit und Raum; zusammen mit einer Sonnenscheibe ist es zu einem beeindruckenden Schmuckstück vereint.[91] Von gesellschaftlich hochstehenden Persönlichkeiten werden an besonderen Festtagen darüber hinaus kronenartige Stirn- und Kopfschmuckstücke oder Brustanhänger getragen, auf denen sich nach oben gerichtete Mondsicheln befinden.

Westafrika
Auch in Westafrika ist Schmuck bekannt, der die Gestirne zum Gegenstand hat. Die Aschanti und Baule – zu den Akan-Völkern gehörende Ethnien im Gebiet von Ghana und der Elfenbeinküste – pflegen bis zum heutigen Tage eine reiche Goldkultur (besonders deutlich wird dies bei den aufwändigen Zeremonien der regionalen Stammeskönige). Bereits im 19. Jahrhundert lassen

137 Tolima-Kultur, Tumbaga-Pektorale, Kolumbien, vorkolumbianisch, Gold, Privatsammlung. Tumbaga pectoral, Tolima style, Columbia, Pre-Columbian, gold, private collection

sich hier goldene Scheiben mit Sonnensymbolen nachweisen, die beispielsweise Bestandteil prächtiger Ketten waren. Darüber hinaus existieren Anhänger in der Form von Mondsicheln sowie goldene Sterne, die unter anderem auf den Kopfbedeckungen der Mitglieder vornehmster Familien getragen werden (Abb. 136).[92]

Amerika
Auch die Indianer Nordamerikas – die Pawnee und Shawnee in Oklahoma und die Seminolen in Florida – benutzen Gestirne als Motive in ihrem Silberschmuck.[93] Besonders hervorzuheben sind die sogenannten Squashblossom-Halsschmuckstücke der Navajos in New Mexico, deren *Naja*-Anhänger möglicherweise auf die frühen Mondsicheln altorientalischer Kulturen zurückgeführt werden können.[94]

Bei den alten Kulturen Südamerikas hingegen scheinen die Gestirne im Schmuck keine oder zumindest nur eine geringe Rolle gespielt zu haben. Das ist sicher bemerkenswert, denn Inti, der Sonnengott der Inka, konnte als goldene Scheibe mit menschlichem Antlitz dargestellt werden, da Gold bei den Inka generell eine bedeutende Stellung einnahm und ein südamerikanisches Märchen die Entstehung von Gold und Silber „erklärt" (s. S. 32). Die anthropomorphen Goldfiguren der Tolima-Kultur Kolumbiens allerdings haben zum Teil wohl einen Bezug zur Sonne. Das legt beispielsweise ein in der Literatur als *Solar bird-man* bezeichnetes Exemplar nahe (Abb. 137).[95]

Ob in Amerika oder der islamischen Welt, ob in Südostasien oder Westafrika: Überall auf der Welt werden die Gestirne geachtet und verehrt, und in vielen Kulturen sind ihre Zeichen zu Motiven im Schmuck geworden.

impressive piece of jewellery.[91] Moreover, persons of high social rank wear forehead and head jewellery or pectoral pendants with crescent moons that open upwards on them on special feast days.

West Africa

In West Africa, too, jewellery is known to have the heavenly bodies as its subject. The Ashanti and Baule – ethnic groups belonging to the Akan peoples who live in Ghana and Côte d'Ivoire – still have a culture rich in gold (this becomes particularly apparent in the elaborate ceremonies associated with regional tribal kings). Gold discs with sun symbols, which were part of magnificent necklaces from here, have been dated to the nineteenth century. There are also pendants in the form of crescent moons as well as gold stars, which members of the leading families wear on their headgear and on other parts of their apparel (Fig. 136).[92]

The Americas

The Native Americans of North America – the Pawnee and Shawnee in Oklahoma and the Florida Seminoles – also used the heavenly bodies as motifs in their silver jewellery.[93] Particularly noteworthy in this connection are the squash-blossom necklaces made by the Navajos in New Mexico. Their *naja* pendants may just possibly derive from the early crescent moons of ancient Near Eastern cultures.[94]

Among the ancient civilisations of Central and South America, on the other hand, the heavenly bodies seem to have played no role at all, or at best a minor one. This is certainly odd because Inti, the Inca sun good, was represented as a gold disc with a human countenance and gold generally occupied an important place in Inca culture. A South American fairy tale 'explains' the creation of gold and silver (see p. 33). Some of the anthropomorphic gold figures of the pre-Columbian Tolima culture of Colombia probably do have a link with the sun, on the other hand. This is suggested for one thing by a figure called a 'solar bird man' in specialist publications (Fig. 137).[95]

Whether in North and South America, the Islamic world, South East Asia or West Africa: the heavenly bodies were respected and venerated throughout the world, and in many cultures signs for them became motifs used in jewellery.

UHREN

Sehr oft handelt es sich bei den Taschen-, Anhänge- und Armbanduhren um echte Schmuckstücke. Ebenso bei den kleinen tragbaren Sonnenuhren, die über Jahrhunderte hinweg in Gebrauch waren. Es scheint daher angebracht, den Zeitmessern, deren Funktion sich ganz konkret auf den Lauf der Sonne und zum Teil auch des Mondes bezieht, ein eigenes Kapitel zu widmen.

Sonnenuhren

„Mach es wie die Sonnenuhr, zähl die heitren Stunden nur". So sagt es ein deutsches Sprichwort und verbindet die Sonne mit den angenehmen Seiten des Lebens. Zwar ist dieser Zusammenhang nicht immer gegeben, tatsächlich ist das Instrument doch nur bei Sonnenschein einsetzbar. Sein sogenanntes Gnomon, ein aufgestellter Stab, wirft dann einen Schatten auf die Erde. Indem dieser über eine Skala wandert, lässt sich der Ablauf der Zeit nachvollziehen. Die Sonnenuhr gilt als das älteste Gerät zur Zeitmessung überhaupt und war schon bei den Ägyptern, in Mesopotamien, im alten Griechenland und in Rom bekannt.[96]

Im Laufe der Jahrhunderte wandelte sich die Sonnenuhr in Form und Gestalt. Sie wurde an Wänden und Türmen angebracht, was zur Folge hatte, dass sie weithin sichtbar war. Die Menschen hatten nun Anhaltspunkte, nach denen sie ihren Tagesablauf gliedern und organisieren konnten.

Die zunehmende Individualisierung des Menschen weckte darüber hinaus den Bedarf an Zeitmessern für den privaten Gebrauch. So schuf etwa Hans Tucher im späten 16. Jahrhundert in Nürnberg zierliche Sonnenuhren aus Elfenbein mit

138 Siegelring mit erzherzoglichem Wappen und Ringsonnenuhr, Süddeutschland (Nürnberg?), um 1524/25, Gold, Bergkristall, Spuren von farbigem Kaltemail, H 3 cm, Dm 2,8 cm. Signet ring with archducal crest and ring sun dial, southern Germany (Nuremberg?), c.1524/25, gold, rock crystal, traces of cold enamel, H 3 cm, dia. 2.8 cm. KHM-Museumsverband, Wien, Inv. KK 2183

139 Taschensonnenuhr, Süddeutschland (?), um 1750, Silber. Pocket sun dial, southern Germany (?), c.1750, silver. Schmuckmuseum Pforzheim, Inv. 1957/80

140 Astronomische Uhr am Altstädter Rathaus von Prag, 1410. Astronomical clock at the Altstädter City Hall in Prague, 1410

WATCHES

Pocket-, pendant- and wristwatches are very often genuine pieces of jewellery. So, too, are the little portable sundials that were used for centuries. Hence it would seem appropriate to devote a chapter to the timepieces whose function is directly related to the course of the sun and also in part to that of the moon.

Sundials

'Do it like the sundial, count only the happy hours.' So goes a German proverb that links the sun with the pleasant sides of life. This may not always be the case, because the instrument can really only be used when the sun is shining. Only then can the part of it called a gnomon, an upright rod, cast a shadow on the ground. In moving across a scale, the shadow of the gnomon marks the passage of time. The sundial is believed to be the oldest instrument of all for measuring time and was known in ancient Egypt, Mesopotamia, ancient Greece, and Rome.[96]

Down through the centuries the sundial changed in form and design. It was attached to walls and towers, which had the effect of making it visible from a distance. Now people had points of reference for structuring and organising their daily routine.

Moreover, the growing individualisation of the human being in society gave rise to a desire for timepieces to be used at need for private purposes. Hans Tucher, for instance, created delicate sundials made of ivory with coloured engraving and metal mounts and fittings in late sixteenth-century Nuremberg. They had several dials, a feature that, along with other incorporated functions, made it possible to define solar and lunar calendars. What had originally been a large sundial had become a sophisticated small work of art that the owner could conveniently carry about on his or her person.[97] This development ultimately led to pieces of jewellery in small formats, such as gold finger rings with dials and a gnomon that could be set up hidden away beneath pop-up hinged covers boasting the owner's coat of arms.[98] Telling time must have been quite difficult with one particular sundial fingerring, however, because the hour scale on this one is housed inside the golden shank of the ring itself (Fig. 138).

Throughout the eighteenth century, small portable sundials in silver with engraved decoration featuring the Baroque acanthus and foliate arabesques were used to tell time and location. Equipped with pop-up gnomons, which were usually triangular in form, they possessed a compass for taking one's bearings from the watch (Fig. 139).[99]

Astronomical clocks

In the late Middle Ages and the early Renaissance, interest in the heavenly bodies not only increased but was linked with great advances in the sciences and growing knowledge of mechanical processes, too. Unsurprisingly, the fifteenth and sixteenth centuries saw the production of extremely complex and aesthetically richly decorated mechanical total works of art, known as astrological clocks. Famous examples that have survived are in sacred buildings such as the Marienkirche in Danzig and Strasbourg Cathedral and some are on the façades of secular public buildings such as the

farbigen Gravuren und Metallbeschlägen. Sie trugen mehrere Zifferblätter, die es neben anderen Funktionen auch ermöglichten, Sonnen- und Mondkalendarien zu bestimmen. Die ursprünglich große Sonnenuhr war zum raffinierten Kleinkunstwerk geworden, das der Besitzer mühelos bei sich tragen konnte.[97] Diese Entwicklung führte schließlich zu kleinformatigen Schmuckstücken, goldenen Fingerringen etwa, deren Zifferblätter und aufstellbarer Schattenstab sich unter Klappdeckeln mit den Wappen der Besitzer verbargen.[98] Die Zeitbestimmung mag bei einem anderen Sonnenuhr-Fingerring allerdings recht kompliziert gewesen sein, ist bei diesem die Stundenskala doch im Inneren der goldenen Ringschiene angebracht (Abb. 138).

Auch im 17. und 18. Jahrhundert dienten kleine tragbare Sonnenuhren aus Silber mit gravierten Ornamenten in barockem Akanthusblatt- und Rankenwerk zur Zeit- und Ortsbestimmung. Sie waren mit aufklappbaren Schattenstäben in meist dreieckiger Gestalt versehen und besaßen einen Kompass zur richtigen Positionierung der Uhr (Abb. 139).[99]

Astronomische Uhren

Im späten Mittelalter und in der Frührenaissance nahm nicht nur das Interesse an den Gestirnen zu, es verband sich auch mit enormen Fortschritten in den Wissenschaften und mit zunehmenden Kenntnissen im Bereich mechanischer Vorgänge. So entstanden im 15. und 16. Jahrhundert höchst komplizierte und künstlerisch reich ausgestattete mechanische Gesamtkunstwerke, sogenannte astronomische Uhren. Prominente Beispiele haben sich in Sakralbauten wie der Danziger Marienkirche und im Straßburger Münster, aber auch an Fassaden profaner öffentlicher Gebäude wie dem Prager Rathaus erhalten (Abb. 140). In einem raffinierten Zusammenspiel von Figuren, Zahlen und Zeichen wurden dem Betrachter die Bewegungen der Gestirne vor Augen geführt und die Himmelsmechanik des damals bekannten Kosmos zum Erlebnis gebracht.

Anhänger-, Taschen- und Armbanduhren

Parallel verlief seit dem 16. Jahrhundert die Entwicklung und Herstellung kunstvoll ausgestatteter Hals- und Taschenuhren, die mit immer zahlreicheren Funktionen aufwarteten. Durch fensterartige Öffnungen im Zifferblatt wanderten nun die Sonne und der Mond, zuweilen auch Wolken, die Wettererscheinungen symbolisierten (Abb. 142). Wie bei den Sonnenuhren achtete man darauf, dass nicht nur praktische Zwecke erfüllt, sondern auch ästhetische Gesichtspunkte berücksichtigt wurden. So kamen etwa in der Zeit des Klassizismus und des Empire sorgfältig gestaltete Uhrgehäuse in Mode, die das nächtliche Firmament mit seinen

141 Dante Gabriel Rossetti, Entwurf für eine Uhr mit den Porträts Rossettis und seiner Frau als Sonne und Mond, 1862, ausgeführt von Cozens, Matthews & Thorpe, London (Nr. 9667). Dante Gabriel Rossetti, watch design with portraits of Rossetti and his wife as the sun and moon, 1862, made by Cozens, Matthews & Thorpe, London (No. 9667)

Altstädter City Hall in Prague (Fig. 140). The sophisticated interplay of figures, numerals and signs showed viewers the movements of the stars and planets and made the celestial mechanics of the universe, as far as then known, an exciting and illuminating experience.

Pocket-, pendant- and wristwatches

In a parallel development since the sixteenth century, ingeniously equipped watches worn from the neck and pocket watches boasted ever more functions. The sun and the moon, occasionally even clouds symbolising weather phenomena, moved visibly through window-like openings in the dials of these timepieces (Fig. 142). As was the case with sundials, attention was paid to ensuring that not only were practical purposes fulfilled but that aesthetic considerations were also taken into account. Carefully designed watch cases featuring the nocturnal firmament became fashionable neo-Classical and Empire accessories: minute diamonds set in a dark blue enamel night sky adorn the back covers of these watches (Fig. 143).

An extraordinary pocket watch has been particularly well documented yet has been lost and will probably remain so.[100] Dante Gabriel Rossetti, poet, painter and illustrator, was probably the most distinguished and versatile founding

142   Thomas Kewell, Taschenuhr mit Übergehäuse, London, um 1690, Messing, feuervergoldet, Weißmetall, Schildpatt, Gold, H 2,7 cm, Dm 4,6 cm (Uhr). Thomas Kewell, pocket watch with casing, London, *c.*1690, brass, fire-gilded, white alloy, tortoiseshell, gold, H 2.7 cm, dia. 4.6 cm (watch). Taschenuhrensammlung Philipp Weber, Leihgabe der Kunststiftung der Sparkasse Pforzheim Calw

143 Jean-Henri David Vauchez, Goldemail-Taschenuhr, Paris, 1789, Messing, feuervergoldet, Email, Glas, Perlen, Diamanten, H 1,6 cm, Dm 5,5 cm. Jean-Henri David Vauchez, gold enamelled pocket watch, Paris, 1789, brass, fire-gilded, enamel, glass, pearls, diamonds, H 1.6 cm, dia. 5.5 cm. Taschenuhrensammlung Philipp Weber, Leihgabe der Kunststiftung der Sparkasse Pforzheim Calw

Sternen zeigen: Kleine Diamanten im dunkelblau emaillierten Nachthimmel zieren ihre rückseitigen Deckel (Abb. 143).

Eine im Kontext der Himmelskörperdarstellung besonders außergewöhnliche Taschenuhr ist zwar hervorragend dokumentiert, doch blieb sie bislang verschollen.[100] Dante Gabriel Rossetti, der wohl prominenteste Vertreter der präraffaelitischen Kunst und Dichtung, entwarf sie nach dem Tod seiner Ehefrau Elizabeth Siddal (Abb. 141). Auf ihrem Zifferblatt stellte der Künstler seine Frau als Luna, sich selbst als Sol dar. Eingebunden in die Dichtung des von Rossetti hoch verehrten Dante Alighieri, ist die Uhr beeindruckendes Zeugnis einer als „kosmisch" verstandenen Liebe, die über den Tod hinausreicht.

Weitaus weniger von Emotionen beeinflusst sind die jüngsten Generationen von Mondphasenchronometern, die gegenwärtig von einigen Uhrenmanufakturen hergestellt werden (Abb. 144). Höchste Präzision und eine aufwändige Mechanik machen es möglich, dass unterschiedliche Zeitzonen, Kalendarien und die Mondphasen sowohl der nördlichen als auch der südlichen Hemisphäre angezeigt werden können. Diese Meisterwerke moderner Uhrmacherkunst stehen in der Tradition ihrer „Vorfahren" seit dem 16. Jahrhundert. Doch geht es heute weniger um die Sichtbarmachung kosmischer Gesetzmäßigkeiten als vielmehr um das jahrtausendealte Bedürfnis nach Selbstdarstellung, das heißt des Schmückens.

member of the Pre-Raphaelite Brotherhood. He produced the design for a watch after the death of his wife, Elizabeth Siddal (Fig. 141). On the face of this watch, made by Cozens, Matthews & Thorpe of London, the artist portrayed his wife as Luna and himself as Sol. Associated with the poetry of Dante Alighieri, whom Rossetti so admired, this commemorative watch provides moving testimony to a love viewed as 'cosmic', transcending death.

The most recent generations of moon-phase chronometers produced by some distinguished contemporary makers of watches are far less influenced by the emotions (Fig. 144). Extremely precise and elaborate mechanical movements now make it possible to show the different time zones, calendars and phases of the moon for both the northern and the southern hemispheres. These contemporary masterpieces of modern watch-making continue the tradition established by their 'forebears' in the sixteenth century. However, the need for personal display – that is, adornment – has outlasted the millennia to claim precedence nowadays over the scientific visualisation of the laws of the universe.

144   Arnold & Son, Mondphasenchronometer *HM Double Hemisphere Perpetual Moon*, 2016, blau lackiertes, guillochiertes Zifferblatt mit blau lackierter, guillochierter Mondphasenscheibe mit goldenen Sternen und zwei gravierten Monden, Handaufzug, 18 Karat-Rotgoldgehäuse, Dm 4,2 cm.   Arnold & Son, *HM Double Hemisphere Perpetual Moon* phase of the moon timepiece, 2016, lacquered blue, guilloched clock face, guilloched moon phase with gold stars and two engraved moons, manual wind, 18 ct red gold casing, dia. 4.2 cm.
Juwelier Leicht, Pforzheim / Arnold & Son, La Chaux-de-Fonds

ANMERKUNGEN

1. Der Koloss von Rhodos, eine ca. 30 Meter hohe Bronzestatue, war dem Helios gewidmet. Um 292 v. Chr. errichtet, stürzte er bereits um 226 in Folge eines Erdbebens ein. Der Koloss zählte in der Antike zu den Sieben Weltwundern und diente im 19. Jahrhundert wohl als Vorbild für die Freiheitsstatue in New York.
2. Zitiert nach Ausst.-Kat. 1996, S. 6
3. Vgl. Ausst.-Kat. 1996 S. 6, 24 ff., 90 ff. und 38 ff.
4. Gen 1,16
5. Vgl. etwa Ps 136,8–9
6. Ps 148,3
7. Ps 84,11
8. Mt 2,2 und 2,6
9. Offb 12,1–2
10. Offb 22,16
11. Sure 7,54
12. Zitiert nach http://peter-schindler.de
13. Prolog im Himmel, Verse 243–246; Zweiter Teil, Verse 4955, 4959, 4965–4966
14. Zitiert nach Bachmann 2009, S. 30
15. Alle Märchen zitiert nach Uther 2000
16. Zum Sonnengesang des Echnaton vgl. Bayer 2007
17. Im italienischen Original wird von *frate sole* (Bruder Sonne) und *sora luna* (Schwester Mond) gesprochen, da dort die Sonne männlich und der Mond weiblich ist. der Lobgesang des Franziskus wurde u.a. von Franz Liszt, Carl Orff und Sofia Gubaidulina vertont.
18. Erstmals veröffentlicht in *Merkur. Deutsche Zeitschrift für europäisches Denken*, Jg. 10, Heft 6 (Juni 1956), S. 534
19. Abgebildet in Singh/Dani 1993, S. 41
20. Abgebildet in Dalmases/Giralt-Miracle 1985, S. 122
21. Jean-Baptiste Lully komponierte 1653 die Musik für das *Ballett Royal de la Nuit*, in dem der junge König als aufgehende Sonne auftrat.
22. Zu diesem Werk siehe „Der Thron des Großmoguls", in: Syndram 2008, S. 108–117, Abb. S. 112/113
23. Abgebildet in Livingston 1970, S. 61, Tafel XXVII
24. Abgebildet in Hughes 1964, S. 159
25. Abgebildet in Aldred 1971, S. 107, vgl. dort auch S. 222
26. Abgebildet in Wilkinson 1972, Farbtafel VIII. Auf manchem ägyptischen Schmuckstück ist zu erkennen, dass auch der Mond zuweilen von einer Barke getragen wird.
27. Abgebildet in Aldred 1971, S. 50, vgl. dort auch S. 187
28. Abgebildet in Maxwell-Hyslop 1971, Tafel 116, vgl. dort auch S. 147
29. Abgebildet in Maxwell-Hyslop 1971, Tafeln 61–64, vgl. dort auch S. 88 ff.; abgebildet auch in Singh/Dani 1993, S. 176
30. Abgebildet in Maxwell-Hyslop 1971, Abb. 130, vgl. dort auch S. 178
31. Abgebildet in Ausst.-Kat. 1995b, S. 259
32. Abgebildet in Kilunovskaya/Semenov 1995, Nr. 261, ohne Seitenangabe
33. Abgebildet in Singh/Dani 1993, S. 282
34. Abgebildet in Singh/Dani 1993, S. 94
35. Die Scheibe befand sich im modernen Kunsthandel, vgl. Royal-Athena-Galleries 2002
36. Augusto Pio Castellani nahm dieses Schmuckstück in der zweiten Hälfte des 19. Jahrhunderts zum Vorbild für eine Brosche, vgl. Abb. 80
37. Abgebildet in Ausst.-Kat. 1995b, S. 137
38. Abgebildet in De Juliis/Alessio/D'Amicis 1986, S. 231, Nr. 161
39. Abgebildet in Gregorietti 1969, S. 119
40. Vgl. hierzu auch Shore 1972, z. B. Abb. 2
41. Abgebildet in Singh/Dani 1993, S. 303
42. Abgebildet in Eichhorn-Johannsen/Rasche/Bähr 2013, S. 51
43. Zur Kultur der Etrusker vgl. Vacano 1957
44. Zur Granulation allgemein vgl. Wolters 1983
45. Abgebildet in Cahn International 2008, S. 65
46. Abgebildet in Haedeke 2000, Nr. 83, S. 66
47. Abgebildet in Wolters 1983, S. 211; vgl. hierzu die detaillierten Informationen von Svetlana S. Rjabzeva in *Juwelirnoje Iskusstvo i Materialnaja Kultura*, Sankt Petersburg 2006, S. 128 ff.
48. Haedeke, Hanns-Ulrich, „Ringe mit Mondsichel und Stern", bislang unveröffentlichtes Manuskript, 2016
49. Abgebildet in Gregorietti 1969, S. 165
50. Abgebildet in Ausst.-Kat. 2008b, S. 109/110
51. Auch Giottos Stern von Bethlehem auf dem Fresko der Anbetung in der Arenakapelle in Padua (1304–06) stellt wohl den Halleyschen Kometen dar, ebenso wie eine Stickerei auf dem Teppich von Bayeux (um 1070).
52. Abgebildet in Munn 2001, S. 47
53. Abgebildet in Ausst.-Kat. 2003a, S. 105
54. Abgebildet in Ausst.-Kat. 1995a, S. 35
55. Abgebildet in Ausst.-Kat. 1999, S. 208
56. Erst Jahrzehnte später entdeckte Howard Carter das Grab des Pharao Tutanchamun, in dem zahlreiche Schmuckstücke mit Darstellungen des heiligen Käfers gefunden wurden.
57. Abgebildet in Munn 2001, S. 342
58. Abgebildet in Nadelhofer 1984, S. 75, sowie in Munn 2001, S. 381
59. Abgebildet in Armstrong 1973, S. 252
60. Im Kreml-Museum in Moskau befindet sich eine Uhr, bei der es sich vermutlich um das nicht fertiggestellte Fabergé-Exemplar handelt.
61. Viele andere Uhren mit Monden und Sternen aus dem Hause Fabergé sind abgebildet in Ausst.-Kat. 2003a, z.B. S. 184/185
62. Vgl. hierzu Possémé, Evelyne et al., „Die Zigarettenetuis von Luzarche d'Azay im Musée des Arts Décoratifs in Paris", in: Ausst.-Kat. 2003a, S. 132 ff.

NOTES

1. The Colossus of Rhodes, an approx. thirty-metre-high bronze statue, was dedicated to Helios. Erected around 292 BC, it had already collapsed by around 226 as a result of an earthquake. In antiquity the Colossus is one of the Seven Wonders of the World and in the nineteenth century doubtlessly served as a model for the Statue of Liberty in New York.
2. English translation quoted in http://oll.libertyfund.org/titles/cicero-on-the-nature-of-the-gods
3. See Ausst.-Kat. 1996, pp. 6, 24 ff., 90 ff. and 38 ff.
4. Gen. 1:16
5. See, for example, Ps. 136:8–9
6. Ps. 148:3
7. Ps. 84:11
8. Matt. 2:2 and 2:6
9. Rev. 12:1–2
10. Rev. 22:16
11. Sura 7, v. 54; English translation quoted in http://corpus.quran.com/translation.jsp?chapter=7&verse=54
12. Quoted in http://peter-schindler.de
13. 'Prologue in Heaven', verses 243–246; Part II, verses 4955, 4959, 4965–4966; English translation quoted in http://www.poetryintranslation.com/PITBR/German/FaustIProl.htm; http://www.poetryintranslation.com/PITBR/German/FaustIIActIScenesItoVII.htm
14. Quoted in Bachmann 2009, p. 30
15. All fairy tales quoted in Uther 2000
16. On the 'Great Hymn to the Aten' see Bayer 2007; English translation quoted in https://ecworlddynamics.wikispaces.com/file/view/Great+Hymn+to+the+Aten.pdf
17. English translation quoted in https://en.wikipedia.org/wiki/Canticle_of_the_Sun; in the Italian original, *Frate sole* (Brother Sun) and *sora luna* (Sister Moon) are spoken of, for there the sun is male and the moon female. The 'Canticle of the Sun' by St Francis of Assisi was set to music by, among others, Franz Liszt, Carl Orff and Sofia Gubaidulina.
18. First published in *Merkur. Deutsche Zeitschrift für europäisches Denken*, Issue 10, No. 6 (June 1956), p. 534 (More beautiful than the remarkable Moon and its ennobled light, / More beautiful than the stars, the celebrated orders of Night, / Far more beautiful than a comet's fiery flight / And called to far more beautiful things than any other star, / Because your life and mine depend on it every day, is the Sun. / Beautiful Sun who rises, who has not neglected her work.)
19. Illustrated in Singh/Dani 1993, p. 41
20. Illustrated in Dalmases/Giralt-Miracle 1985, p. 122
21. In 1653 Jean-Baptiste Lully composed the music for *Ballett Royal de la Nuit*, in which the young king performed as the rising sun.
22. On this work see 'Der Thron des Großmoguls', in: Syndram 2008, pp. 108–117, Fig. pp. 112–113
23. Illustrated in Livingston 1970, p. 61, plate XXVII
24. Illustrated in Hughes 1964, p. 159
25. Illustrated in Aldred 1971, p. 107, see also p. 222
26. Illustrated in Wilkinson 1972, colour plate VIII. On some Egyptian jewellery pieces, the moon can occasionally be seen being carried by a boat.
27. Illustrated in Aldred 1971, p. 50, see also p. 187
28. Illustrated in Maxwell-Hyslop 1971, plate 116, see also p. 147
29. Illustrated in Maxwell-Hyslop 1971, plates 61–64, see also pp. 88 ff.; illustrated also in Singh/Dani 1993, p. 176
30. Illustrated in Maxwell-Hyslop 1971, Fig. 130, see also p. 178
31. Illustrated in Ausst.-Kat. 1995b, p. 259
32. Illustrated in Kilunovskaya/Semenov 1995, No. 261, unpaginated
33. Illustrated in Singh/Dani 1993, p. 282
34. Illustrated in Singh/Dani 1993, p. 94
35. The disc can be found on the modern-day art market, see Royal-Athena-Galleries 2002
36. In the second half of the nineteenth century Augusto Pio Castellani took this piece of jewellery as a model for a brooch, see Fig. 80
37. Illustrated in Ausst.-Kat. 1995b, p. 137
38. Illustrated in De Juliis/Alessio/D'Amicis 1986, p. 231, No. 161
39. Illustrated in Gregorietti 1969, p. 119
40. On this, see also Shore 1972, e.g. Fig. 2
41. Illustrated in Singh/Dani 1993, p. 303
42. Illustrated in Eichhorn-Johannsen/Rasche/Bähr 2013, p. 51
43. On Etruscan culture see Vacano 1957
44. On granulation in general see Wolters 1983
45. Illustrated in Cahn International 2008, p. 65
46. Illustrated in Haedeke 2000, No. 83, p. 66
47. Illustrated in Wolters 1983, p. 211; on this see the detailed information by Svetlana S. Rjabzeva in *Juwelirnoje Iskusstvo i Materialnaja Kultura*, Saint Petersburg 2006, pp. 128 ff.
48. Haedeke, Hanns-Ulrich, 'Ringe mit Mondsichel und Stern', hitherto unpublished manuscript, 2016
49. Illustrated in Gregorietti 1969, p. 165
50. Illustrated in Ausst.-Kat. 2008b, pp. 109–110
51. Giotto's Star of Bethlehem on the fresco of the Adoration in the Arena Chapel in Padua (1304–06) indeed also portrays Halley's Comet, as does an embroidery on the Bayeux Tapestry (c.1070).
52. Illustrated in Munn 2001, p. 47
53. Illustrated in Ausst.-Kat. 2003a, p. 105
54. Illustrated in Ausst.-Kat. 1995a, p. 35
55. Illustrated in Ausst.-Kat. 1999, p. 208
56. Not until decades later did Howard Carter discover the tomb of the pharaoh Tutankhamun, in which

63 Abgebildet in Ausst.-Kat. 1981, Nr. 287
64 Abgebildet in Ward 1981, S. 148
65 Abgebildet als Anzeige der Firma Hancocks, London, in *Jewellery Studies*, volume 1 (1983/84)
66 Das Schmuckstück befindet sich zurzeit im Kunsthandel bei A la Vieille Russie, New York.
67 „Le Luxe de Paris contre le chômage", in: *L'Intransigeant*, 26. Oktober 1932; S. 1/2 (deutsche Übersetzung durch den Verfasser)
68 Auch später blieb das Haus Chanel den Gestirnen treu, was etwa der Armreif *Clair Obscur* beweist; er ist abgebildet in Mauriès 2012, S. 252
69 Abgebildet in Hughes 1964, S. 126
70 Abgebildet in *Jewellery History Today*, issue 3 (September 2008), S. 9
71 Abgebildet in *Wartski Catalogue*, London 2010, Nr. 39
72 „Cartier, qui fait tenir, magicien subtil, de la lune en morceaux sur du soleil en fil"; Jean Cocteau, zitiert nach Nadelhofer 1984, S. 2
73 Abgebildet in Munn 2001, S. 381; vgl. zu Sonnendiademen im 19. Jahrhundert auch Nadelhofer 1984, S. 75 f
74 Abgebildet in Possémé 2012, S. 170
75 Abgebildet in Hughes 1964, S. 205
76 Abgebildet in Hughes 1964, S. 202
77 Abgebildet in Folchini Grassetto 2005, S. 97 und 99
78 Abgebildet in *Jewellery Studies*, volume 4 (1990), S. 83
79 Abgebildet in Krauss 2008, S. 169
80 Abgebildet in Ausst.-Kat. 1995a, S. 274
81 Vgl. hierzu Goring et al. 2008, S. 144 ff.
82 Zu den Ringen von Bernhard Schobinger vgl. Adamson 2014
83 Abgebildet in Falk/Holzach 1999, S. 99, 130 und 141
84 Abgebildet in Fishof 2014, S. 158
85 Abgebildet in Grotenhuis van Onstein 2008, S. 170 ff.
86 Abgebildet in Heiniger 1974, S. 304
87 Zur Schmuckproduktion im Kaukasus vgl. Tortschinskaja/Komlewa 1988, mit zahlreichen Abbildungen
88 Vgl. hierzu auch Sychowa 1984 sowie Frembgen 2015, S. 72
89 Vgl. die Abbildungen in Richter 2000, S. 205–207
90 Vgl. Richter 2000, S. 15
91 Abgebildet in Borel 1996, S. 219
92 Vgl. Ausst.-Kat. 2009, dort auch Angaben zu weiterführender Literatur
93 Vgl. Ausst.-Kat. 1975, mit zahlreichen Abbildungen
94 Frederick Dockstader, ehemaliger Direktor des New Yorker Museum of the American Indian, führt einer mündlichen Aussage zufolge die Naja-Anhänger der Navajos auf altorientalische Lunula-Anhänger zurück, die ihren Weg vom Orient über das islamisch besetzte Spanien und – im 18. und 19. Jahrhundert – über Mexiko zu den Navajos gefunden haben.
95 Vgl. Singh/Dani 1993, S. 33
96 Eine knappe Zusammenfassung der Entwicklung der Zeitmesser findet sich in Thomas/Leiter 1997, S. 10 ff.
97 Abgebildet in Pippa 1966, S. 221
98 Abgebildet in Ward 1981, S. 102
99 Mehrere Exemplare sind abgebildet in Pippa 1966, S. 229
100 Munn, Geoffrey C., „Not lost but gone before: The Story of the Rossetti Watch", in: *The Decorative Arts Society Journal*, No. 35 (2011), S. 34 ff.

numerous pieces of jewellery featuring representations of the sacred beetle were found.
57 Illustrated in Munn 2001, p. 342
58 Illustrated in Nadelhofer 1984, p. 75, also in Munn 2001, p. 381
59 Illustrated in Armstrong 1973, p. 252
60 In the Kremlin Museum in Moscow there is a timepiece presumed to be the unfinished Fabergé specimen.
61 Many other timepieces featuring moons and stars from the House of Fabergé are illustrated in Ausst.-Kat. 2003a, e.g. pp. 184–185
62 On this see Possémé, Evelyne et al., 'Die Zigarettenetuis von Luzarche d'Azay im Musée des Arts Décoratifs in Paris', in: Ausst.-Kat. 2003a, pp. 132 ff.
63 Illustrated in Ausst.-Kat. 1981, No. 287
64 Illustrated in Ward 1981, p. 148
65 Shown as an advertisement for the company Hancocks, London, in *Jewellery Studies*, Vol. 1 (1983/84)
66 The jewellery piece can be currently found on the art market at A la Vieille Russie, New York.
67 'Le Luxe de Paris contre le chômage', *L'Intransigeant*, 26 October 1932, pp. 1–2
68 Later the House of Chanel too remained true to the firmament, as demonstrated, for example, by the *Clair Obscur* cuff; this is illustrated in Mauriès 2012, p. 252
69 Illustrated in Hughes 1964, p. 126
70 Illustrated in *Jewellery History Today*, Issue 3 (September 2008), p. 9
71 Illustrated in *Wartski Catalogue*, London 2010, No. 39
72 'Cartier, qui fait tenir, magicien subtil, de la lune en morceaux sur du soleil en fil'; Jean Cocteau, quoted in Nadelhofer 1984, p. 2
73 Illustrated in Munn 2001, p. 381; on sun diadems in the nineteenth century see also Nadelhofer 1984, pp. 75–76
74 Illustrated in Possémé 2012, p. 170
75 Illustrated in Hughes 1964, p. 205
76 Illustrated in Hughes 1964, p. 202
77 Illustrated in Folchini Grassetto 2005, pp. 97 and 99
78 Illustrated in *Jewellery Studies*, Vol. 4 (1990), p. 83
79 Illustrated in Krauss 2008, p. 169
80 Illustrated in Ausst.-Kat. 1995a, p. 274
81 On this see Goring et al. 2008, pp. 144 ff.
82 On the rings by Bernhard Schobinger see Adamson 2014
83 Illustrated in Falk/Holzach 1999, pp. 99, 130 and 141
84 Illustrated in Fishof 2014, p. 158
85 Illustrated in Grotenhuis van Onstein 2008, pp. 170 ff.
86 Illustrated in Heiniger 1974, p. 304
87 On jewellery production in the Caucasus see Tortschinskaja/Komlewa 1988, with numerous illustrations
88 On this see also Sychowa 1984 and Frembgen 2015, p. 72
89 See the illustrations in Richter 2000, pp. 205–207
90 See Richter 2000, p. 15
91 Illustrated in Borel 1996, p. 219
92 See Ausst.-Kat. 2009, and also information there on further literature
93 See Ausst.-Kat. 1975, with numerous illustrations
94 According to an oral account, Frederick Dockstader, former director of the New York Museum of the American Indian, can trace the *naja* pendants of the Navajo back to ancient Oriental lunula pendants, which found their way from the Orient via Islamic-occupied Spain and – in the eighteenth and nineteenth centuries – via Mexico to the Navajos.
95 See Singh/Dani 1993, p. 33
96 A short summary on the development of the timepiece can be found in Thomas/Leiter 1997, pp. 10 ff.
97 Illustrated in Pippa 1966, p. 221
98 Illustrated in Ward 1981, p. 102
99 Further examples are illustrated in Pippa 1966, p. 229
100 Munn, Geoffrey C., 'Not Lost but Gone Before: The Story of the Rossetti Watch', *The Decorative Arts Society Journal*, No. 35 (2011), pp. 34 ff.

DANK

Der erste und vornehmste Dank gilt Anna Vladimirovna Ratnikova, die als für den Schmuck zuständige Mitarbeiterin des Russischen Museums für Ethnographie in Sankt Petersburg die Anregung gegeben hat, sich mit den Gestirnen als Motiven zur Gestaltung von Schmuckstücken zu befassen. Cornelie Holzach als Leiterin des Schmuckmuseums Pforzheim und ihren Mitarbeiterinnen Sabina Eckenfels, Katja Poljanac und Isabel Schmidt-Mappes danke ich für die wunderbare Möglichkeit, diese Ausstellung und das Begleitbuch zu realisieren. Das Museum ist und bleibt die erste Adresse, um Schmuck auf einzigartige Weise zu präsentieren.

Das Team von Arnoldsche Art Publishers in Stuttgart – mit Dirk Allgaier als Verleger, mit Marion Boschka, die das Buch in seiner Gesamtheit betreut hat, mit Silke Nalbach, von der das Layout stammt, und mit Winfried Stürzl, der mit großem Einfühlungsvermögen für das Lektorat verantwortlich zeichnet – hat keine Mühe gescheut, die vorliegende Publikation zu ermöglichen. Allen gebührt besonderer Dank.

Unzählige Personen – Museumsdirektorinnen und -direktoren, Kuratorinnen und Kuratoren, Restauratorinnen und Restauratoren, Registratorinnen und Registratoren, Fotografinnen und Fotografen, Kunsthändlerinnen und Kunsthändler, Schmuckkünstlerinnen und Schmuckkünstler, Sammlerinnen und Sammlern im In- und Ausland – haben alle dazu beigetragen, dass dieses Buch und die Ausstellung *Himmlisch. Sonne, Mond und Sterne im Schmuck* realisiert werden konnten. Sie können hier nicht alle namentlich genannt werden. Allen möchte ich für ihre Unterstützung meinen Dank aussprechen.

Fritz Falk

ACKNOWLEDGEMENTS

First of all we should like to acknowledge our indebtedness to Anna Vladimirovna Ratnikova, who, as the jewellery curator at the Russian Museum for Ethnography in Saint Petersburg, was the one to make the suggestion that we should concern ourselves with the heavenly bodies as motifs used in the design of jewellery. I thank Cornelie Holzach as director of the Pforzheim Jewellery Museum and her colleagues, Sabina Eckenfels, Katja Poljanac and Isabel Schmidt-Mappes, for providing us with the wonderful opportunity of organising this exhibition and publishing the book to accompany it. The Jewellery Museum is, and will remain, the prime venue for presenting jewellery in a unique setting.

The Arnoldsche Art Publishers team in Stuttgart – Dirk Allgaier as publisher, Marion Boschka, who has accompanied the book from start to finish, Silke Nalbach, who designed the layout, and Winfried Stürzl, who has shown such empathy in editing it – have spared no efforts in making the present publication possible. To all of you we are grateful indeed.

Countless people – museum directors, curators, conservationists, registrars, photographers, art dealers, jewellery artists, and collectors, home and abroad – have all contributed to realising this book and the exhibition *Heavenly. The Sun, Moon and Stars in Jewellery*. They cannot all be named here. I would like to express my thanks to all of them for their support.

Fritz Falk

LITERATUR IN AUSWAHL / SELECTED BIBLIOGRAPHY

Adamson, Glenn, *Bernhard Schobinger. The Rings of Saturn*, Stuttgart 2014

Aldred, Cyril, *Jewels of the Pharaohs. Egyptian Jewellery of the Dynastic Period*, London 1971

Armstrong, Nancy, *Jewellery. An Historical Survey of British Styles and Jewels*, Guildord 1973

Bachmann, Hans-Gert, *Mythos Gold. 6000 Jahre Kulturgeschichte*, München 2009

Battke, Heinz, *Geschichte des Ringes. In Beschreibung und Bildern. Dargestellt durch die Sammlung Battke*, Baden-Baden 1953

Bayer, Christian, *Echnaton – Sonnenhymnen*, Stuttgart 2007

Bellinger, Gerhard J., *Knaurs Lexikon der Mythologie. Mit über 3000 Stichwörtern zu den Mythen aller Völker*, München 1999

Birnie-Dansker, Jo-Anne (ed.), *Jugendstil-Gürtelschließen. Die Sammlung Kreuzer / Art Nouveau Buckles. The Kreuzer Collection*, Stuttgart 2000

Borel, France, *Ethnos. Gioielli da terre lontane della collezione di Colette e Jean-Pierre Ghysels*, Milano 1996

Bott, Gerhard, *Ullstein-Juwelenbuch. Abendländischer Schmuck von der Antike bis zur Gegenwart*, Frankfurt a. M./Wien 1972

Breitling, Günter et al., *Das Buch vom Gold*, Luzern/Frankfurt a.M. 1975

Cahn International AG, Auktionskatalog, September 2008, Basel 2008

Cahn's Quarterly, 2/2013 (Basel 2013)

Chadour-Sampson, Anna-Beatriz and Rüdiger Joppien, *Schmuck. Kunstgewerbemuseum der Stadt Köln*, 2 vols., Köln 1985

Cristofani, Mauro and Gabriele Cateni, *L'or des Ètrusques*, Paris 1985

Dalmases, Núria de and Daniel Giralt-Miracle, *Plateros y joyeros de Cataluña*, Barcelona 1985

De Juliis, Ettore M., Arcangelo Alessio and Amelia D'Amicis, *Les ors hellénistiques de Tarente*, Milano 1986

Deppert-Lippitz, Barara, *Griechischer Goldschmuck*, Mainz 1985

Drutt English, Helen, *Brooching it Diplomatically. A Tribute to Madeleine K. Albright*, Stuttgart 1998

Drutt English, Helen, *Peter Skubic. BETWEEN*, Stuttgart 2001

Du Ry, Carel J., *Völker des Alten Orient (Kunst im Bild)*, Baden-Baden 1969

Eichhorn-Johannsen, Maren, Adelheid Rasche and Astrid Bähr (eds), *25 000 Jahre Schmuck. Aus den Sammlungen der Staatlichen Museen zu Berlin*, Berlin 2013

Falk, Fritz and Cornelie Holzach, *Schmuck der Moderne. Bestandskatalog der modernen Sammlung des Schmuckmuseums Pforzheim*, Stuttgart 1999

Fishof, Iris, *Jewellery in Israel. Multicultural Diversity. 1948 to the Present*, Stuttgart 2014

Flower, Margaret, *Victorian Jewellery*, London 1967

Folchini Grassetto, Graziella, *Contemporary Jewellery. The Padua School*, Stuttgart 2005

Frembgen, Jürgen Wasim, *Töchter der Steppe, Söhne des Windes. Gold und Silber der Turkmenen*, München 2015

Glüber, Wolfgang, *Jugendstilschmuck. Der Bestand im hessischen Landesmuseum Darmstadt*, Regensburg 2011

Goring, Elizabeth, et al., *Kevin Coates. A Hidden Alchemy. Goldsmithing, jewels and table-pieces*, Stuttgart 2008

Gregorietti, Guido, *Il gioello nei secoli*, Milano 1969

Greiffenhagen, Adolf, *Schmuckarbeiten in Edelmetall*, 2 vols., Berlin, 1970–1975

Grotenhuis van Onstein, Vinciane van, *Diamond Divas*, Schoten 2008

Haedeke, Hanns-Ulrich and Marion Menniken, *Schmuck aus drei Jahrtausenden. Sammlung Hanns-Ulrich Haedeke*, Köln 2000

Heiniger, Ernst A., Jean Heiniger and Eduard Gübelin, *The Great Book of Jewels*, Lausanne 1974

Higgins, Reynold A., *Greek and Roman Jewellery*, London 1961

Hughes, Graham, *Modern Jewellery 1890–1961*, London 1964[2]

Kalter, Johannes, Ursula Didoni and Almuth Seltmann, *Schmuck aus Nordafrika*, Stuttgart 1976

Kern, Anne-Barbara, *Fabergé Ei-Objekte aus der Manufaktur Victor Mayer / Fabergé Eggs by Victor Mayer*, Stuttgart 2015

Kilunovskaya, Marina and Vl. A. Semenov (eds.), *The Land in the Heart of Asia*, St. Petersburg 1995

Kostjuk, Olga G., *Masterpieces of European Jewellery from the 16th to 19th Centuries in the Hermitage Collection*, St. Petersburg 2010

Krauss, Günter, *GünterKrauss.Schmuck*, Stuttgart 2008

Leiter, Alfred, Alma Helfrich-Dörner and Günter Meyer, *Email-Uhren. Kostbarkeiten unter den Taschenuhren*, Kornwestheim 1978

Livingston, Linda (ed.), *Dali. A Study of his Art-in-Jewels. The Collection of the Owen Cheatham Foundation at the Virginia Museum of Fine Arts*, New York 1970

Ludwig, Reinhold, *Schmuck 2000. Rückblick, Visionen*, Ulm 1999

Ludwig, Reinhold, *Schmuckdesign der Moderne. Geschichte und Gegenwart*, Stuttgart 2008

Marquardt, Brigitte, *Schmuck. Realismus und Historismus 1850–1895, Deutschland, Österreich, Schweiz*. München/Berlin 1998

Mauriès, Patrick, *Jewelry by Chanel*, London 2012

Maxwell-Hyslop, Rachel, *Western Asiatic Jewellery. Circa 3000–612 B.C.*, London 1971

Meylan, Vincent, *Boucheron. The Secret Archives*, Woodbridge 2011

Munn, Geoffrey C., *Castellani and Giuliano. Revivalist Jewellers of the 19th Century*, New York 1984

Munn, Geoffrey C., *Tiaras. A History of Splendour*, Woodbridge 2001

Nadelhofer, Hans, *Cartier. König der Juweliere*, Herrsching am Ammersee 1984

Neubecker, Ottfried, *Heraldik. Wappen, ihr Ursprung, Sinn und Wert*, Frankfurt a.M. 1977

Perry, Jane, *Traditional Jewellery in Nineteenth-Century Europe*, London 2013

Pippa, Luigi, *Masterpieces of Watchmaking*, vol. I, Lausanne 1966

Possémé, Évelyne (ed.), *Van Cleef & Arpels. L'art de la haute joaillerie*, Paris 2012

Richter, Anne, *Jewelry of Southeast Asia*, New York 2000

Royal-Athena-Galleries, *Art of the Ancient World*, vol. XIII, New York/London 2002

Schöner, Hans (Hg.), *90 Jahre Zünfte. Gestaltung im Wandel der Zeit. Arbeiten von Zünftlern in der Zeit von 1912–2004*, Königsbach-Stein 2004

Seibert, Ilse, *Die Frau im alten Orient*, Leipzig 1973

Shore, Arthur F., *Portrait Painting from Roman Egypt*, revised edition, London 1972

Singh, Madanjeet and Ahmad Hasan Dani, *The Sun. Symbol of Power and Life*, New York 1993

Sychowa, Natalya, *Traditional Jewellery from Soviet Cenral Asia and Kazakhstan*, Moscow 1984

Syndram, Dirk, *Juwelenkunst des Barock. Johann Melchior Dinglinger im Grünen Gewölbe*, München 2008

Tait, Hugh, *Jewellery through 7000 Years*, London 1975

Tait, Hugh, and Charlotte Gere, *The Art of the Jeweller. A catalogue of the Hull Grundy Gift to the British Museum. Jewellery, engraved gems and goldsmith's work*, 2 vols, London 1984

Thomas, Uta and Alfred Leiter, *Taschenuhren. Sammlung Philipp Weber, Pforzheim*, Pforzheim 1997

Torbrügge, Walter, *Europäische Vorzeit (Kunst im Bild)*, Baden-Baden 1968

Tortschinskaja, Elga and Galina Komlewa, *Juweliererzeugnisse*, Ethografisches Museum der Völker der UdSSR, Leningrad 1988

Uther, Hans-Jorg (ed.), *Die schönsten Märchen zu Sonne, Mond und Sternen*, München 2000

Vacano, Otto Wilhelm von, *Die Etrusker in der Welt der Antike*, Reinbek bei Hamburg 1957

Vever, Henri, *La bijouterie française au XIXe siècle*, 3 vols, Paris 1906–1908 (Vever, Henri, *French Jewellery from the 19th Century*, translated from the French by Katherine Purcell, London 2001)

Wallis, Rosemary Ransome, Worshipful Company of Goldsmiths, *Treasures of the 20th Century. Silver, jewellery and art medals from the 20th century collection of the Worshipful Company of Goldsmiths*, London 2000

Wamser, Ludwig and Rupert Gebhard (eds), *Gold. Magie, Mythos, Macht. Gold der Alten und Neuen Welt*, Stuttgart 2001

Ward, Anne et al., *Rings through the Ages / Der Ring im Wandel der Zeit*, München 1981

Werlich, Uta and Susanne Germann, *Inrô. Japanese Belt Ornaments / Gürtelschmuck aus Japan. The Trumpf Collection*, Stuttgart 2016

Wilkinson, Alix, *Ancient Egyptian Jewellery*, London 1972

Willis, Roy (ed.), *Mythologie*, Köln 2006

Wolters, Jochem, *Granulation. Geschichte und Technik einer alten Goldschmiedekunst*, München 1983

Ausstellungskataloge in Auswahl / Selected exhibition catalogues

Ausst.-Kat. 1975: *Silberschmuck nordamerikanischer Indianer aus der Sammlung des Museums of the American Indian, New York*. Schmuckmuseum, Pforzheim. Pforzheim 1975

Ausst.-Kat. 1978: *Zierkämme und ornamentaler Haarschmuck aus Japan aus der Sammlung Chiyo Okazaki, Tokio*. Schmuckmuseum, Pforzheim. Texts by Fritz Falk. Pforzheim 1978

Ausst.-Kat. 1980: *Tutanchamun*. Haus der Kunst, München. Mainz 1980

Ausst.-Kat. 1981: *Volkstümlicher Schmuck aus Italien aus der Sammlung des Museo Nazionale delle Arti e Tradizioni Popolari*, Rom. Schmuckmuseum, Pforzheim. Texts by Fritz Falk. Pforzheim 1981

Ausst.-Kat. 1984a: *Sieraden. En lichaamsversiering uit Indonesië*. Volkenkundig Museum Nusantara, Delft. Delft 1984

Ausst.-Kat. 1984b: *Silberschmuck aus Ägypten*. Galerie Exler & Co., Frankfurt a.M. Edited by Helga Exler-Bachinger, texts by Richard Bachinger and Peter W. Schienerl. Frankfurt a.M. 1984

Ausst.-Kat. 1986: *Fabergé. Hofjuwelier der Zaren*. Kunsthalle der Hypo-Stiftung, München. Edited by Géza von Habsburg. München 1986

Ausst.-Kat. 1988: *InrĐ. Gürtelschmuck des Japaners aus Beständen des Linden-Museums Stuttgart*. Schmuckmuseum Pforzheim. Texts by Werner Weissbrodt. Pforzheim 1988

Ausst.-Kat. 1993: *Fabergé. Imperial Jeweller*. State Hermitage Museum, St. Petersburg, Musée des Arts décoratifs, Paris, Victoria and Albert Museum, London. Edited by Géza von Habsburg and Marina N. Lopato. London 1993

Ausst.-Kat. 1995a: *Sieraad symbool signaal. The jewel – sign and symbol*. Koningin Fabiolazaal, Antwerp. Edited by Jan Walgrave. Antwerp 1995

Ausst.-Kat. 1995b: *Unterwegs zum Goldenen Vlies. Archäologische Funde aus Georgien*. Museum für Vor- und Frühgeschichte, Saarbrücken. Edited by Andrei Miron and Mixeili Abramišvili. Stuttgart 1995

Ausst.-Kat. 1995c: *Zarengold. 100 Meisterwerke der Goldschmiedekunst aus der Staatlichen Eremitage St. Petersburg*. Schmuckmuseum Pforzheim. Edited by Fritz Falk and Olga Kostjuk. Stuttgart 1995

Ausst.-Kat. 1996: *Zwischen Himmel und Erde. Allumfassend – Das Joanneum*. Landesmuseum Joanneum, Graz. Edited by Thomas Höft. Graz 1996

Ausst.-Kat. 1999: *Tiffany Retrospective. Designs from Tiffany & Co. 1837–1999*. Mitsukoshi Museum of Art. Texts by Vivienne Becker et al. Tokyo 1999

Ausst.-Kat. 2003a: *Fabergé – Cartier. Rivalen am Zarenhof*. Kunsthalle der Hypo-Kulturstiftung, München. Edited by Géza von Habsburg et al. München 2003

Ausst.-Kat. 2003b: *Jewellery from Renaissance to Art Déco 1540–1940*. Tokyo Metropolitan Teien Art Museum, Fukuoka City Museum, Matsusakaya Art Museum, Nagoya, Art Museum Eki, Kyoto. Texts by Diana Scarisbrick and Akio Seki. Fukuoka 2003

Ausst.-Kat. 2003c: *The Splendour of Diamond: 400 Years of Diamond Jewellery in Europe*. The National Museum Tokyo, 2003, Municipal Museum, Osaka, 2004. Edited by Jan Walgrave. Tokyo 2003.

Ausst.-Kat. 2007: *Tiara. Dignity and Beauty. The Story of the Tiara*. The Bunkamura Museum of Art, The Niigata Bandajima Art Museum, The Museum of Tokyo. Texts by Diana Scarisbrick. Tokyo 2007

Ausst.-Kat. 2008a: *The Art of Gem Engraving. From Alexander the Great to Napoleon III*. The Hakone Open-Air Museum, Fukuoka, Fukuoka City Museum. Texts by Diana Scarisbrick et al. Fukuoka 2008

Ausst.-Kat. 2008b: *Brilliant Europe: Jewels from European Courts*. Belgique SA Espace Culturel, Bruxelles. Edited by Diana Scarisbrick. Bruxelles 2008

Ausst.-Kat. 2009: *Gold in der Kunst Westafrikas*. Helvetisches Goldmuseum, Schloss Burgdorf, Galerie Walu, Zürich. Edited by Jean David and Jane David. Zürich 2009

BILDNACHWEIS / PHOTO CREDITS

Die Ziffern sind Abbildungsnummern. The figures given are illustration numbers.

VG Bild-Kunst, Bonn 2016: Gijs Bakker, Jean Lurçat, Bernhard Schobinger, Peter Skubic

Collection A. Aardewerk Antiquair Juwelier, The Hague, The Netherlands: 97
De Agostini Picture Library / Bridgeman Images: 140
De Agostini Picture Library / G. Dagli Orti / Bridgeman Images: 5, 34, 35
De Agostini Picture Library / G. Nimatallah / Bridgeman Images: 45
Courtesy by Albion Art: 62, 74
Archäologische Staatssammlung München, Bildnr. GD 2000-266, Foto © M. Eberlein: 38
Archiv Arnoldsche Art Publishers: 94, 114
Arnold & Son: 144
Photo Les Arts Décoratifs, Paris / Jean Tholance. Tous droits réservés: 88–91, 101, 103, 108
Badisches Landesmuseum Karlsruhe, Foto Thomas Goldschmidt: 52, 133
Günter Beck: 142, 143
Photo © Boltin Picture Library / Bridgeman Images: 27, 137
Collection Alain Boucheron: 105
bpk: 16
bpk / adoc-photos: 63
bpk / Margarete Büsing: 24
bpk / Herbert Kraft: 41
bpk / Ägyptisches Museum und Papyrussammlung, SMB / Stefan Büchner: 39
bpk / Ägyptisches Museum und Papyrussammlung, SMB / Margarete Büsing: 1
bpk / Antikensammlung, SMB / Johannes Laurentius: 3
bpk / Bayerische Staatsgemäldesammlungen: 50
bpk / BnF, Dist. RMN-GP: 20
bpk / Deutsches Historisches Museum / Sebastian Ahlers: 9
bpk / Kupferstichkabinett, SMB / Jörg P. Anders: 14, 49
bpk / Nationalgalerie, SMB / Jörg P. Anders: 12
bpk / RMN – Grand Palais / Daniel Arnaudet: 6
bpk / RMN – Grand Palais / Hervé Lewandowski: 36
bpk / RMN – Grand Palais / René-Gabriel Ojéda: 28
bpk / RMN – Grand Palais / Mathieu Rabeau: 30
bpk / RMN – Grand Palais / Franck Raux: 29, 31
bpk / Staatliche Kunstsammlungen Dresden / Jürgen Karpinski: 54
bpk / Staatliche Kunstsammlungen Dresden / Hans-Peter Klut: 23
Bridgeman Images: 8
© The Trustees of the British Museum. All rights reserved: 40, 55, 71, 80, 81, 136
© Jean-David Cahn AG, Basel: 37

CHANEL Joaillerie: 105
© Chaumet: 84
Attai Chen: 124
Chopard Deutschland: 126
© Kevin Coates, Image © National Museums Scotland: 117
© The Fitzwilliam Museum, Cambridge: 2
© Photo courtesy of the Foundation Silvio Denz, © Christie Mayer Lefkowith, *The Art of René Lalique flacons and powder boxes*, photographer Skot Yobauje: 21
Hessisches Landesmuseum Darmstadt, Foto Wolfgang Fuhrmannek: 98, 99
H-P. Hoffmann Düsseldorf: 107
© Foto Petra Jaschke: 67, 118, 121, 128–132, 134, 135
Juweliere Leicht, Pforzheim: 106
KHM-Museumsverband: 22, 48, 138
Kunsthistorisches Museum, Vienna, Austria / Bridgeman Images: 61
© Landesamt für Denkmalpflege und Archäologie Sachsen-Anhalt, Foto Juraj Lipták: 7
© Landesmuseum Württemberg, Foto P. Frankenstein / H. Zwietasch: 46
Library of Congress, Prints and Photographs Division, Miscellaneous Items, LC-DIG-ppmsca-04459 (digital file from original): 70
© Linden-Museum Stuttgart, Foto A. Dreyer: 92
The Link of Times Foundation, St. Petersburg: 87
Victor Mayer & Co KG: 85
Mucha Trust / Bridgeman Images: 100
The Museum of Fine Arts Houston, photograph by Thomas R. DuBrock: 115
Museum of Modern Art, New York, USA / Bridgeman Images: 13
Collection Radius et Margelidon: 69
Menachem Reis: 125
Rheinisches Bildarchiv Köln, Foto Marion Mennicken, rba_d040172_02: 42
© Rijksmuseum, Amsterdam: 66
A. Ruppenthal KG: 127
© Schmuckmuseum Pforzheim, Foto: Rüdiger Flöter: 75, 112, 119
© Schmuckmuseum Pforzheim, Foto Petra Jaschke: 26, 32, 33, 51, 56, 59, 60, 78, 79, 95, 102, 113, 116, 137
© Schmuckmuseum Pforzheim, Foto Günther Meyer: 44, 47
© Foto Helga Schultze-Brinkop: 109, 110
Schweizerisches Nationalmuseum, Foto Nr. DIG-24612: 19
Shuxiu Lin, Musée Lalique, collection Shai Badmann & Ronald Ooi: 93
© Staatliche Antikensammlung und Glyptothek München, Foto Renate Kühling: 43
© Staatliches Museum Ägyptischer Kunst, München, Foto Marianne FrankePhotograph: 25
© The State Hermitage Museum / photo by Vladimir Terebenin: 57, 58
Courtesy of Tadema Gallery, London
Photo © Tallandier / Bridgeman Images: 53
Courtesy of Rupert Wace Ancient Art, London: 4
Wartski, London: 82, 83, 86, 141
© Foto Petra Zimmermann: 120